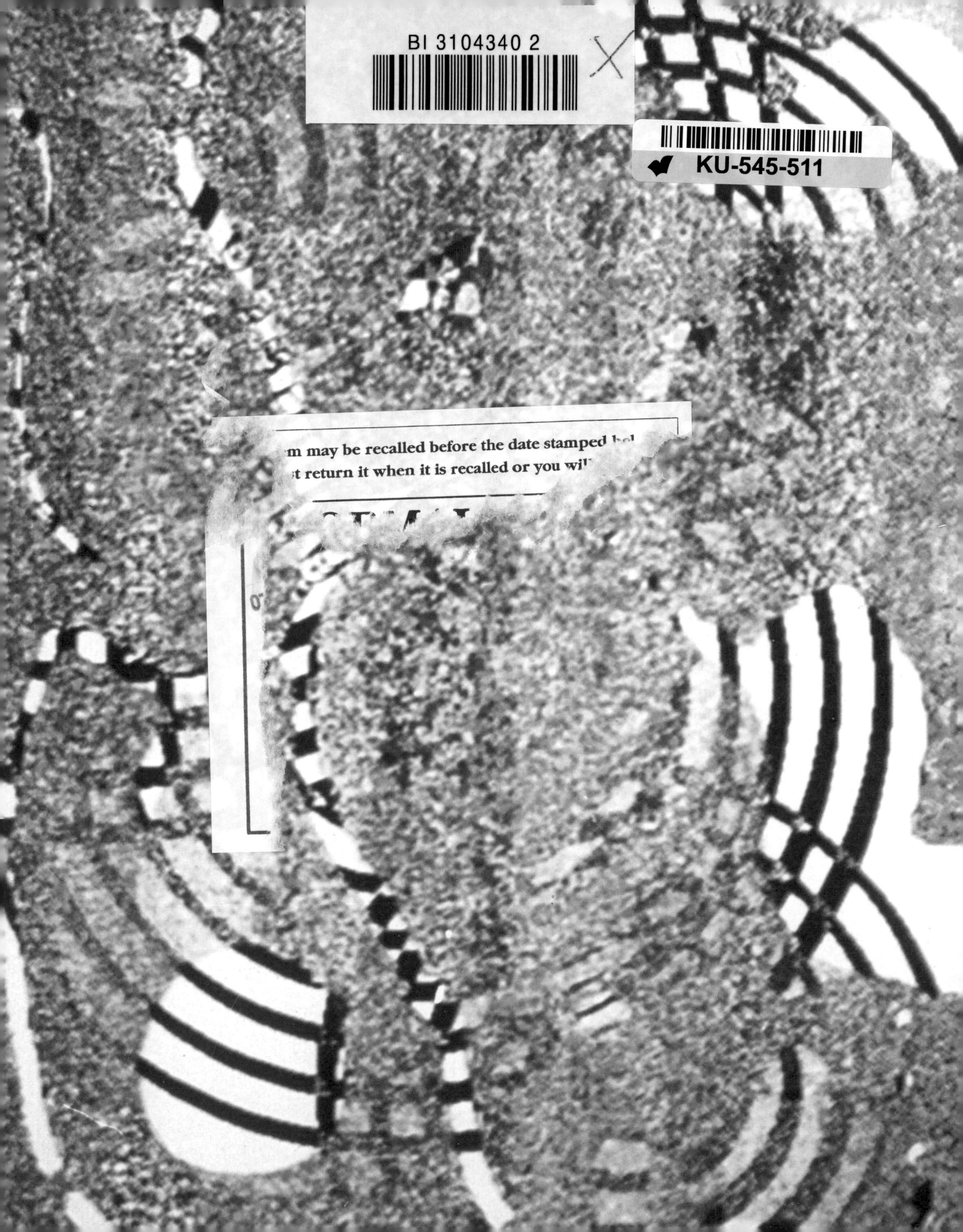

Let's Talk with the World

A Child's Guide to Art and the Natural World

Let's Talk with the World

A Child's Guide to Art and the Natural World

Written by
Karla Cikánová

CRAFTSMAN HOUSE

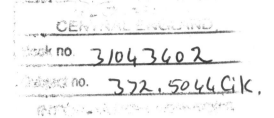
Designed and produced by Aventinum Publishing House,
Prague, Czech Republic

This edition first published in 1998

Distributed in Australia by Craftsman House,
Tower A, 112 Talavera Road,
North Ryde, Sydney, NSW 2113
in association with G+B Arts International:
Australia, Canada, China, France, Germany, India,
Japan, Luxembourg, Malaysia, The Netherlands,
Russia, Singapore, Switzerland, Thailand

ISBN 90 5703 31 19

Written by Karla Cikánová
Translated by Eva Turková

The book presents works by children of the Primary School
in Londýnská Street, Prague, and students of the Faculty
of Education of Charles University, Prague
Instructive drawings and photographs by Karla Cikánová
Photographs in Mini-galleries by Karla Cikánová (in most cases),
Štěpán Aussenberg (p. 30, A), Jiří Kornatovský (p. 31, E),
Vojtěch Písařík (p. 54, A)
Photograph on p. 36 (General Sherman) by Pavla Jiráková
Graphic design by Daruše Singerová

Printed in the Czech Republic
1/99/62/51-01

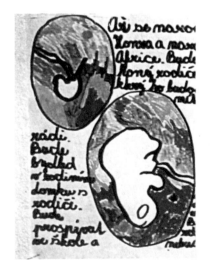

Contents

Preface

Some arguable views expressed by children:

'I wanted a dog, but now I prefer the computer... Dad talks with the computer and is even rude to it... When dad works with the computer I have to be quiet... What I like best are animals on the video... I prefer to draw because it's rather awkward with the mouse... If I don't like the picture I made on the computer I just wipe it out... When I make drawings on the computer, it's as if the pictures are not really mine... The computer knows better than me... It's my best friend... Never mind that I am dead, I have another three lives in the computer... I don't get dirty when I work with the computer and don't make a mess...'

It is clear that the quality of a child's relationship with whatever they encounter is influenced by their parents and, later, by the people they meet. We know that from our own childhood and teenage experience. There are natural activities which help to develop perception, the emotional and rational cognition of the world in which a child must find its place. Creative activity is one of them.

Pencils, crayons, twigs, fingers and brushes, which it is possible to draw and paint with, were suddenly joined by the mouse, a new device which makes everything easier and faster, and the computer which can offer the little artists graphic programs. The children were not surprised; the teachers were taken aback, enthusiastic or anxious. (Some parents like to leave their child with the computer where it is quiet, no questions are asked and the child is suspended in a kind of 'timelessness'.)

Among the people a child meets is somebody who puts a pencil or brush in their hand or who, for the first time, switches on the computer in front of the child. In both cases the person should remain available for the child to talk to, knowing why and what the child draws or paints with a brush or a mouse, and when and where to use a computer. The person should keep company with the child, explain, disclose and help to search for the mysteries of the world, disclose them and help to search, point out the beauty of a stone, tree, flying bird, the human body – all this is part of the person's duty, responsibility and care. In how a child reflects the stars, clouds, stones, trees, birds or people in their creative expressions, we can find not only the child, but also ourselves.

The media, TV, video or the computer cannot make decisions for us. They help to broaden our senses but we still remain human beings. While we identify with them to a greater or lesser extent, however, we still become part of them through the electronic monster, the all-embracing robot that today's civilisation has almost become; a place where information multiplies. Are we able to handle this situation?

Our fifth publication on creative activities for children from the age of eight offers a broad range of means of expression – drawing, painting, collage, the creative reshaping of maps, work with photocopies and slides, the creation of space and computer graphics. All the creative activities are subject-interlinked in five chapters, which deal with the sensual, emotional and rational contacts with the 'universe', 'plants', 'animal species', 'man' and 'that which after generations remains of permanent value'. Present in all chapters is also communication, the human ability to search for and find answers to the question of our place under the stars and on the planet. The tool itself – pencil, brush or computer mouse – cannot create a dandelion, a portrait, a landscape full of light, the spring rain or the dream of a flying horse. It is a living person, a child, who tries to reflect in a creative language his/her emotional relation to reality or how it is conceived.

All creative activities are preceded by touches of reality, evoked memories, ideas and dreams. And what stops us from staying with the children and their emotional experiences of the sky at night, the flash of lightning, the flight of butterfly or stork, the smell of a meadow, the song of a bird or person? That it is just as possible to stop in surprise in front of a huge tree, a blade of grass between paving stones or rocks, as in front of a work of art, is illustrated by our mini-gallery at the end of every chapter.

The time we spend with the children and the computer will be short, proportionate to the task, which this fast-working machine can easily accommodate. Together we can try quick variations, phasing, metamorphoses etcetera: the growth of a crystal or shell, the colourful changes of the seasons, the changes of human moods, animated discussions, reconciliation or the stages of a quarrel.

It has been found that the computer, carefully chosen and directed towards a suitable subject, can surprisingly demonstrate by the picture we created on the monitor that we are part of Nature and not of a technical super-machine, created by humankind.

The reason why this fifth book was written is simple but urgent. Did you notice? Everyone talks a lot and quotes Fromm's wise words: 'It is better to be than to have.' We constantly personify Nature: 'If you destroy me, you shall perish!' But in the meantime some students of the technical faculty decide to change the car into an electromobile or helimobile, an ecologist puts a fence around a threatened nature reserve, another ecological movement saves the whale. Every day a teacher considers how to motivate children so that when drawing a blade of grass, the shell of a snail or the wings of a butterfly they realise how fragile the whole of nature on our planet is, of which humankind is an indivisible part.

Fears that all human existence could perish gave rise to cultures which watched the universe from monumental observatories and temples, looking for whoever made them. Urgent fears concerning human existence in our time can lead to the creation of a spiritual and rational culture, which responsibly places in front of civilisation the task of tidying up and recycling all that endangers the natural life of plant and animal communities on this planet.

Don't you think that this is also a task for teachers? Don't laugh. It should be clear to future scientists, politicians, economists and philosophers that it is not possible to live a poor existence on a pile of material/technical rubble and find pleasure only in exceptional human rationality, the substitutional virtual reality of a video about Nature without Nature. Whether our fifth book, which came about with the help of not only the children of the primary school in Londýnská Street in Prague, but also students of the Faculty of Education of Charles University, can contribute to a better understanding, sensitivity, knowledge and wisdom is for you to judge.

Karla Cikánová

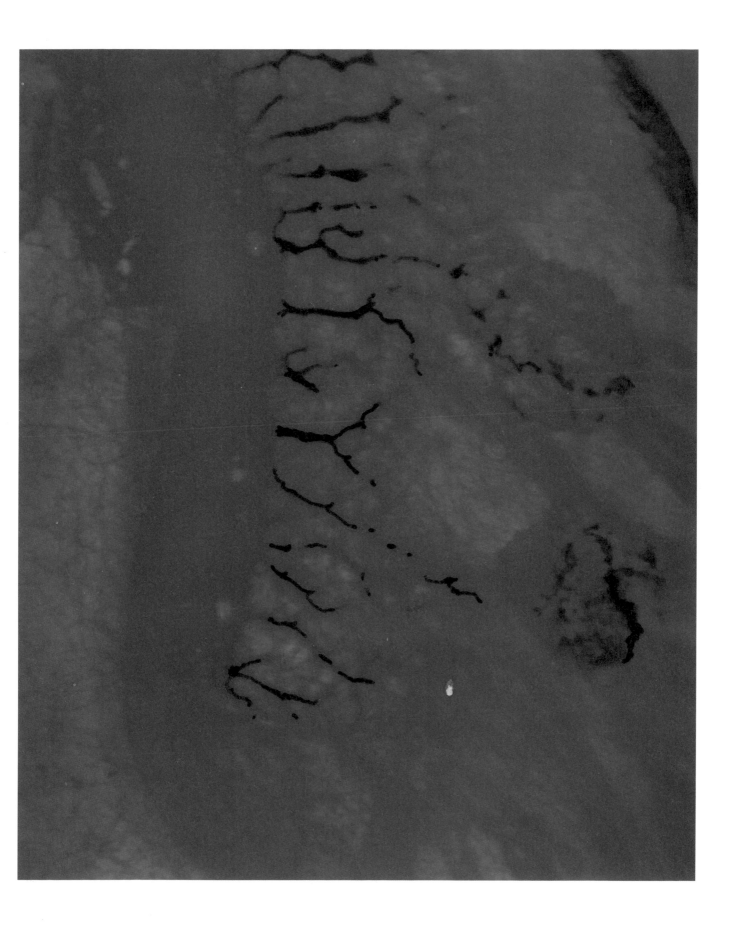

1

1

2

Let Us Imagine Our Place in the Universe

How to make time visible? About the Big Bang. Galaxies, stars and planets. Flying over our planet. Fantastic mapping. The energy of the elements.

Humankind, as compared, let's say, to a happy dolphin, is endowed with worries. We are the only animal species on this planet which asks: 'Where did I come from? Why am I here? Why am I as I am? How long will I be here?' In rare moments, both layperson and scientist admit that when looking into the macro-world of the universe or the micro-world of nuclear particles, their head spins. We still do not know anything accurate about the beginning and the end or the infinitude of the existing world.

Space and time, their limits or infinitude, are explained in the history of humankind, by numerous myths, religions and rational scientific discoveries. But any time a person stands under the sky full of stars, they see and perceive roughly the same thing, but their explanation of the secret of the existence of the world is and always will be different, depending on how much rationality and imagination they find within themselves, drawn from the sum of the universal memory.

Before you continue reading, try to put on paper a short sentence or small picture of what you understand of the word 'time'. You can ask your friends, younger and older children or students to do the same. We shall give you some rather interesting ideas or metaphors from our own collection, then we shall try to put some order into this heterogeneous mix.

1 *Looking for the centre of the cosmos.* The children drew a spiral as if they were discovering new galaxies rotating at a distance of a hundred million light-years. Look at pictures in books about the universe and find the centre from which everything evolves and moves.

2 *The conception of the centre* – the Big Bang – was created on the computer with the help of the KID-PIX program. According to the astronomers the Big Bang occurred 15–20 billion years ago. Here, however, it looks more like a child's creation. It reminds us of the heat of the life-giving Sun. Did the Big Bang know that our planet would need heat, light, water and air? Did it anticipate people?

3

3 *The primal father* who is responsible for everything, the creator, one of the gods? This personification of the universe gave people the chance to live, think and be part of Nature. A mysterious being was created by spreading dry crayons. In its coat it has enough warmth for all living creatures. Two children from the 3rd class worked on a large format.

Time is: 'A thread with knots of events. A trip to an infinite point. A spiral from nothing in the micro-cosmos to nothing in the macro-cosmos and between that there is "something". An empty circle. A tree whose branches become roots of another tree. Time is a cocoon, a ball of thread, a spider walking in circles. Zero on the thermometer. A pulsating core. The beating of a big heart. Sparks in a large brain. A constantly bigger fish eating smaller

4

4 *Janus – January, also the beginning.* It has two faces and looks into the past with one and into the future with the other. But where is the present? Say 'now' very quickly. Did it quickly disappear into the past? Using paper soaked in glue and then put on a balloon, a student created a large head with two faces. Inside, as in a lantern, an 'eternal light' can shine and the head can rotate because it is hollow. It reminds us that we use our head to think about rapidly passing time.

5 a   *The time machine* drawn by smaller children, in the form of a kind of mill, is quite particular. Smoke comes out of its chimney as it struggles through the course of the birth, life and death of people and animals. Their time is measured by a dial and hands. The decomposition of lifeless matter is measured by the hour-glass at the bottom.

5 b   *The cooking stove of time.* This measure of time was created by a boy from plasticine. It is 'mad' and tries to demonstrate Albert Einstein's 1905 statement which overthrew some of the certainties people held on to: 'Time and space are deformed according to how substances move in relation to each other.' In a book for children we might interpret it this way: from the point of view of slower moving bodies, time seems to slow down in faster moving bodies. Children are familiar with sci-fi in which astronauts return from a flight still young because they flew at almost the speed of light.
That is why the boy's creative measure of time can be extended like a piece of elastic.

5 c   *An alarm-clock* which does not let you fall asleep again. The big hand is stopped by a kind of ball, making it impossible to return to the past except in memories. 'Teacher, we read a story in which an astronaut met himself in a time loop. Shouldn't we remove the blue ball so that time can also turn backwards? Do you know how many films there are in which people travel not only to the future, but also to the past?'

 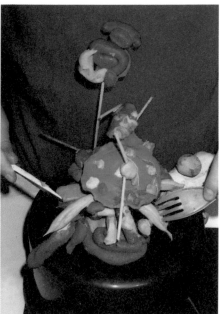

5 a   5 b

and smaller fish. Time is the egg of a big hen. It is grass that survives fire. A crystal that grows inside and outside. Time is the rotation of a cosmic particle. The light of a star which is already dead. Time is a washing machine with bubbles and me inside. A huge mill made by humankind. Time is a museum. A castle. A growing rubbish heap. All the cut beards of wise men. A straight line with an abscissa – life and death. Time is omniscience – a baby in the morning, an old man in the evening ... etcetera.'

I am sure you can tell which ideas were expressed in words and which by

5 c

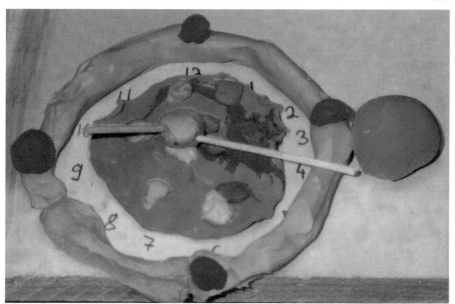

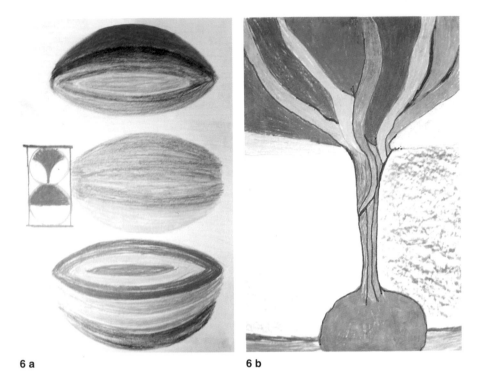

6 a

6 b

6 a *Time as a pulsating core in peel* was drawn by a thirteen-year-old boy with crayons. He sees life as seeds, eggs or a pulsating heart, which turn or vibrate between peels. The boy explained that they protect it from death, keeping it warm or cooler and giving it nutrients. The life of the hot core is limited by the hour-glass, however, and finally the core drops into the dark and cold half of the peel.

6 b *Time as the tree of life,* with earth on its roots, needs light, darkness, warmth, water and nutrients to be able to live. It seems that the earth on the roots is floating in the water in which life was created. This is a picture made by an older girl who explained that the branches could reflect diversity and the evolution of plant and animal species in time.

pictures. If you arrange them according to their similarity you will find that 'time' is perceived either as an infinite straight line or abscissa or, on the contrary, as a cycle – a circle or spiral.

Some ideas come close to ancient myths without the person knowing it. The ideas are supported not only by metaphors and personification, but also

6 e

6 c

6 d

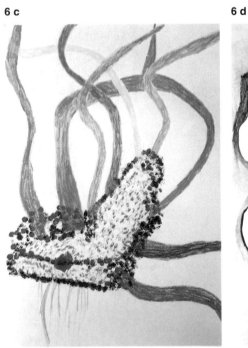

6 e *Time/space for me in the universe.* That is my life.

6 c *The time of my 'self'.* Sometimes it seems that everything is easy, we are happy. At other times we are terribly sad and everything goes wrong. It is as if we had a ribbon of different colours around our head for our different moods. This could also be a kind of record of our condition.

6 d *Time of illness – time of sadness.* This time passes very slowly. 'It's not easy to fall asleep because we only think about bad things and are full of fear and anguish. It's as if you had swallowed a thistle or black spider. We feel as if we are on a desert island.' Those were the impressions the other children gained from the picture.

7 a *Time of changes.* The children tried to illustrate their idea of time with the help of the computer. In the first case it was a mixture of two pleasant seasons – spring and summer. When compared to human life, spring was childhood, summer maturity.

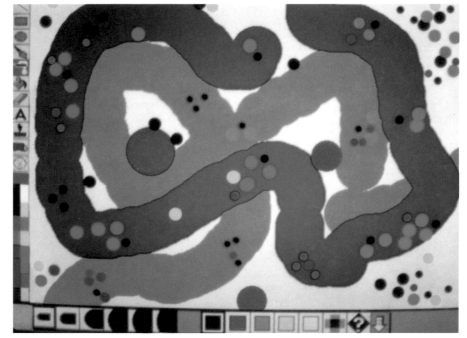

7 a

by geometry, physics, even chemistry and frequently biology. And last but not least, by astronomy.

We then tried to draw or paint on paper or the computer screen (with the help of the KID-PIX graphic program) the fantastic imaginings concerning universal, natural or human time. How successful the older children were can

7 b

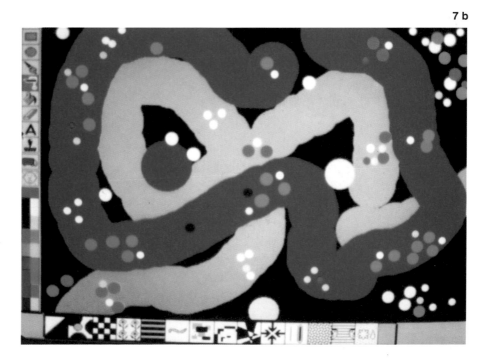

7 b *When they made a negative* they were surprised by the change of colours. The blue they ascribed to autumn – the wise maturity, a ripeness. Grey was winter and old age. And what are the various large coloured points? Significant happy and sad days, months and even the happiest years in life. Perhaps one could put one's own 'secret calendar' in the computer.

8

8 *Routes in the universe.* Everything moves in space, even though we have a feeling of calm and stillness when looking at the night sky. The children tried to draw, with wax crayons, the sum of the routes of cosmic bodies by ellipses or other curves in a kind of 'timetable', then completed the picture with black Indian ink. Let's try to count how often the moon turns around the earth in a year, in a hundred years ...

be seen from their pictures on pages 12–15. They wanted to show something more than chronometers – it was not a question of devices, watches, clocks or alarm clocks. Whether they felt time as a core with a peel, an infinite thread, a spiral of cosmic time/space or a very personal interchange of happiness and sadness, the computer enabled them to give imaginary time movement in contrasting, quick changes, which included 'growing', variations

9 b

9 a

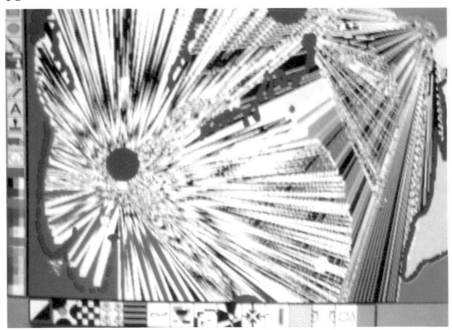

9 a, b *Cosmic radiation.* What signals from the stars can an astrophysicist record with their equipment? Look at some books about the universe. You will find out about trace radiation, what the signals of the radio-galaxies are or what one can read from the various colours of the spectrum, the light of far-away stars. We tried to illustrate the signals by which stars tell us something about themselves, with the help of the KID-PIX program. Even little children draw the heat and light radiating from the sun in the pictures.

10 a *Origin and extinction.* The constant change not only of the universe but of everything we see around us can be illustrated in a quick and interesting way using the graphic program on the computer. The lines can rotate, the galaxies and stars can shine, explode or intertwine. Sometimes it is orderly and tidy and nothing happens for a long time, then suddenly a new star explodes which '... supplies material for the nebula, which contracts, rotates and soon there is another star, our sun. The remaining material turns into independent planets...' (J. Grygar and V. Železný, *Windows to the Universe Wide Open*).

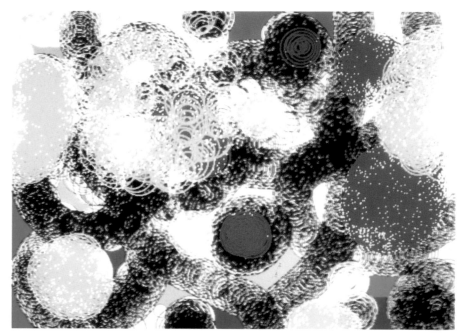

10 a

and phases, enlarging etcetera. I watched two boys draw a complicated coloured spiral with the mouse. They enlarged its centre and brought it closer. They then completed the spiral and again brought its centre closer. They explained that 'digging' into the centre is infinite but their time is not. Let astronauts open up these endless spaces! Other children found that they never complete their infinitely growing tree, crystal, the shell of a snail, the annual

10 b

10 b *Every sunrise* reminds us of the birth of a new star. It is difficult to imagine that our present sun will one day turn into a red giant, a star with a diameter 100 times larger than it is today. Now its diameter is 696,000 km, it shines 400,000 times more than the full moon and is 150 million km (i.e. 8.3 light-minutes) away from us. If we read further about its dimension, weight and energy capacity, we will be surprised. The sun gives life to our earth. Our forefathers considered it a god. This painting by three children celebrates the miracle of the sun.

11 a

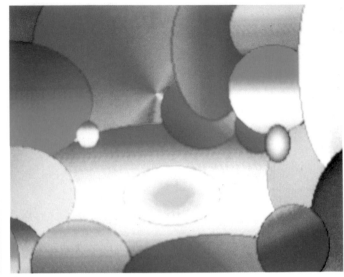

11 b

rings of a tree stump or the carapace of a tortoise that represented their conception of time. It is enough to keep your eyes open and watch it pass in the space around us. To keep the rhythm of time and try to understand its metamorphoses, use the time for something sensible and specific: watch, hear, see, smell, draw, paint, sing, build, appreciate .... Time gives us endless opportunities. Rashness, feverish discoveries and the consumption of constantly new things leads, however, to loss and oblivion. To slow down and sometimes stop leads to a better understanding of things.

11 c

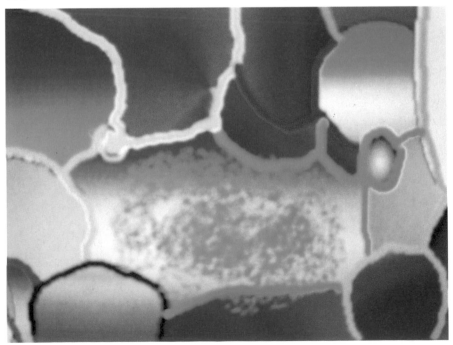

11 a–c *Throughout its existence humankind will make expeditions to endlessness:* the emptiness of time/space that gave birth to the universe. Where did we come from? Why are we here and how long will we be here? Three boys tried to explain this on the computer. If our huge cosmic bubble has four dimensions – one is time and the other three space (height, width, length) – is it possible to imagine, at least in mathematical, physical or creative fantasy, what it looks like in other 'cosmic bubbles' which have ten or more dimensions and other physical properties and elements? Hardly! In this computer phasing carried out by some older children, they 'pushed apart bubbles' of various universes to look at what is behind them, what brought them about and what they will eventually be submerged in. Humankind has a constant dialogue with the macro-cosmos outside and the micro-cosmos inside ourselves. We call the miracle of maxi-creation and mini-creation providence, infinity, endlessness, god, the magic space foam ...

12 a–c *Our vital star – the sun and its nine children.* Planets also have a 'birthday' in the universe. About five billion years ago, a large cloud rotating around its axis moved about in space on the edge of the galaxy. Part of the substance concentrated around the central axis, the rotation and temperature increased, the core started to radiate and our nearest star, the sun, appeared! The original cloud around the sun turned into the planets. What character and temperament do the nine children of the sun have? You can read about it in books and look at pictures, but you can also paint and imagine that some are kind and

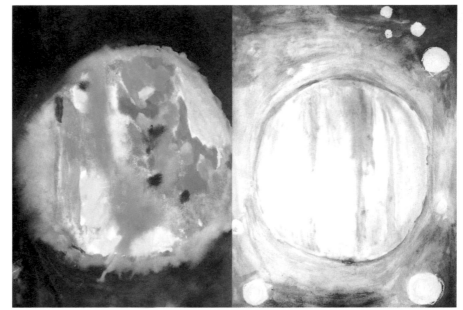

12 a   12 b

And so we shall leave the computer switched off. We shall have a look at that infinity. Let us take a clear summer night, a place somewhere in a meadow, where the stars are not hidden due to the artificial light from a town or city. In the northern hemisphere there are tales about the constellations. The children chose the Big Dipper. We took with us a hard, transparent foil, a felt-tip pen, a torch and a map of the stars. Will we be able to hold the foil and draw the seven stars of the Big Dipper with our felt-tip pen? Did it work? It is pleasant to talk to stars that have a name. They were given their names long before we appeared on the scene and so it seems that we are not only

12 c

12 d

thoughtful, some very happy, and others angry. Let's try to paint the wise blue planet of life; the earth. And what about other ways of imagining it? If people stop appreciating it, will they upset the vital balance of conditions – heat, water and air for the plants, animals and humankind? What would the dead planet look like? What did the children paint?

12 d *Interesting routes, viaducts and underpasses* were created from collages of pictures of the Saturn halo cut out by the children. They used the pieces as in a jigsaw puzzle.

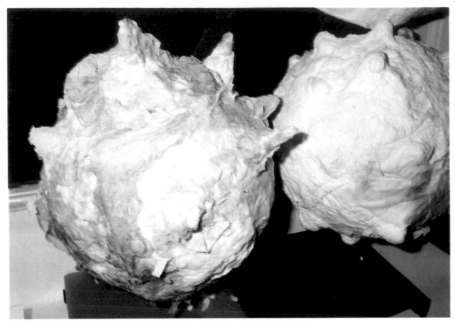

13 a

13 b

13 a, b *Let's make a little planet* to see how much effort it takes. We were lucky enough to get hold of some small globes. We then mixed some glue with water and fixed some cellulose to them. How many mountains, volcanoes and canyons will the planet have? What colours will it have? Don't you think that one of them is like a large chestnut and another like a shrinking, wrinkled nut?

talking with the stars, but also through time with people who looked at them before us and gave them their names. At the end of the shaft of the Big Dipper shines the Benetnash. Then follows the Mizar with a small star above it. This is called Alcor. We tried to unwind the mysterious fact that Mizar is actually composed of six stars, with the help of a small atlas of stars for children. We continue to introduce the stars, moving in the direction of the shaft

13 c

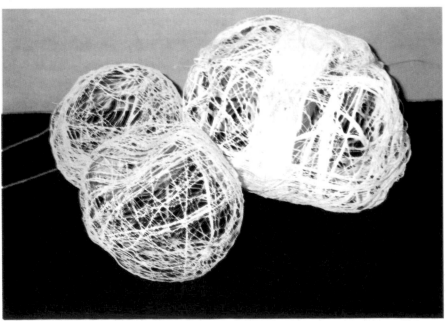

13 c *The orbits of satellites round the planet?* Can they be counted after all these years? There must be a 'flight schedule' and every orbit has its purpose. Have the astronomers drawn them on the round globe? Let's help them. The picture does not just show threads dipped in glue and wound around a balloon or ball. Those hollow balls can be an image of satellite orbits in the children's imagination, a railway station in the universe. Even though this was the work of a student, I am sure that little children would also be able to make a large hollow ball. But look out! Do you know that the earth receives space junk? We saw it marked by a computer on the map of our earth. Where will we put it all? Can the parts of a broken satellite that did not burn up be put on the rubbish heap?

14 *Attention, we are leaving!* So far we have looked out into the universe through our telescope of fantastic ideas. Now let's try to look at the continents from an aeroplane as if we were on an investigative flight. First we made our own plane out of paper, a swallow or an arrow, which we placed under a large white paper posing as the blank sky. By rubbing a dark wax crayon over the paper we made our aeroplane visible. The children then pushed the swallow under the paper and again made every phase visible by rubbing. They then glued their planes on the right side. Almost ten metre long paper strips with the phases of the swallows' flight were then hanging on the staircase by the third floor of our school. These illustrations were for the school exhibition, 'The Earth's Head is Full of Us'.

14

A = Benetnash   D = Megrez
B₁ = Mizar   E = Dubhe
B₂ = Alkor   F = Merak
C = Alioth   G = Phekda

and then clockwise: we can see Alioth, then Megrez, the back part of the Dipper is illuminated by Dubhe, the back wheel consists of Merak and the front wheel is turned by Phekda. Don't these names sound mysterious and beautiful?

Two people may agree on one common star and, at a certain time in the evening, they look at it even if they are far apart. They greet each other through the star; they have their secret bond. (I sometimes say to myself, 'Hello Mizar! Give my love to my grandson. You are our star.') When looking at the stars, the Big Dipper for example, we are seeing them at different depths in the universe. Benetnash is furthest away from the Earth: with the speed of light we would reach it in 163 light-years. Perhaps on a warm summer night we will read something about the stars in our little atlas. Are you

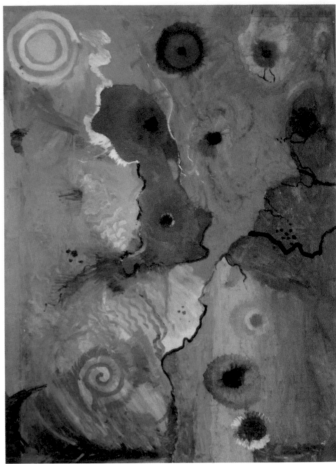

15 a

15 b

fond of the legend of the beautiful princess Callisto, who was changed into a bear? Or perhaps the myth of the Ethiopian queen Cassiopeia? Read some legends to the children. When they go home, they can draw in daylight what they saw at night. For example, they can draw portraits of the stars according to the names of the stars they remember and how those names sound. Mizar could be a choleric warrior, Phekda a wise aunt, and Dubhe perhaps a dreamy princess.

Other magic can be produced with the computer. We have constellations on our foil. If you hold the foil up to the monitor, why not try to draw, with the help of the KID-PIX program, a fantastic picture of the Big Dipper, hitch some horses to it and add a person. If the children drew other constellations, it depends on them how they will complete and colour them on the monitor according to the foil. If there are no more drawings on the foil, why not use the atlas of stars to create other constellations of either the northern or southern night sky? These drawings could be exchanged by fax and then compared. How does a little Australian imagine what the Big Dipper looks like?

When looking at the calm and clear night sky, there is nothing that could remind us of the much discussed 'Big Bang'. When playing with the children, let us illustrate one theory which presumes that our universe was created from some kind of 'bubble'. Surely the astrophysicist will forgive us if, after

15 a, b *Mapping.* From time to time old maps are discarded in schools. We got large maps of the continents for our art lessons. We put our tables together and laid the maps on them. On other tables were pictures of the earth as seen from Apollo 12, and an open book with material on what the continents looked like 280 million years ago: the single floating shape of Pangea. Would it be possible to cut the continents out from a smaller map of the hemisphere and put Pangea together? What did Gondwanaland look like 50 million years later? The continents got their present shape only 130 million years ago. How different did their landscape and surface look then? And so we played around. We shifted mountain ranges, deserts and gulfs on the map. Islands were created. Continents grew or disappeared. Can you tell which map the children drew?

16 a *How we made mixtures with the weather.* Meteorologists must give warnings about tornadoes over the continents, hurricanes over the Atlantic, typhoons in the Pacific and the regions around the Indian Ocean. How do storms, gales and whirlwinds come about? Gales around the eye of a hurricane rotate from 320 to 800 km per hour, and the diameter can be up to 25 km. We read about them and were flabbergasted by their power. Pictures of clouds over the continents and oceans are fascinating. We not only found pictures of tornadoes, but also large posters on which the earth was surrounded by clouds. It was a strange feeling when the children encircled the disintegrating cloudiness with their fingers and tried to push the clouds away with their palms. We are certainly very small, but we still tried to draw and talk about how people themselves are responsible for the weather and even the changes of climate.

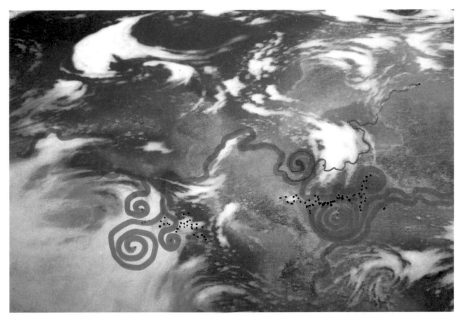

16 a

the children read the description of the Big Bang, they get some shampoo, make bubbles with the help of a tube made from newspaper, and pretend that they are astrophysicists. Let us make a time/space foam. It bubbles and boils. The amount constantly grows, then disappears. Look how the small bubbles are unable to grow. Hardly anyone succeeds in increasing the size of the bubble in that initial 'nothingness'. And then suddenly, perhaps by mistake or due to the froth, something separates, which the astronauts shame-

16 b

16 b *A map of catastrophes* was made after a discussion on the origin of earthquakes and their consequences, tidal waves and volcanic activity. We also talked about the damage caused by nuclear testing, the reasons for the overheating of our planet (global warming), the causes of smog, depletion of ozone and the disappearance of greenery after the senseless, rapid cutting down of forests etcetera. A fantasy painting of the injured planet was made directly on the map. It was as if the ocean had sunk and black cracks threatened Australia, extending to Africa and north as far as Alaska. In the Atlantic Ocean we can see the huge eye of a hurricane. Africa is slowly drowning in poisonous purple water while the Pacific is boiling. And Europe? Europe has long ago disappeared under water. It is only possible to survive in the suddenly warmer Greenland. Is the largest island in the world big enough for all the people left?

17 a

17 a–d *Further mapping.* Several children decided to create their pictures on old maps. Teams of three first discussed what their picture of the world should reflect and which artistic means they would use. The children then added a short legend to their picture.

17 a *Our earth is a mirror of the stars.* (Paintings and prints.) The children explained their picture of the world by saying that, in the same way people make maps of the stars in the sky to determine their place in the universe, stars can also look at themselves in the mirrors of the oceans and seas or even in the smallest body of water such as a well. Try to look at the stars in a body of water such as a pond on a still summer night.

lessly call bubble. The possibility of a future world. And now look out! What was it like, Mr. Astrophysicist Grygar? Fifteen or twenty billion years ago one of those bubbles became separated from the bubbly foam of the space/time ocean. Can you see it? It does not look at all like the other bubbles: it survived. This quantal birth is what scientists call the Big Bang. That is how our universe came about: it spreads, it has a specific composition of space and time coordinates, forces and particles, chemical elements and physical properties, which brought about the origin of our planet and life on it. Don't be sad that you managed only one bubble; you can always conjure up another one.

17 b

17 b *The world is all news.* (Collage made from newspapers and the resulting painting.) The children told us that information about any event spreads rapidly and not only through the press. What else occurred to them when talking about their picture? It's good to know what is going on not only in the antipodes, but also in our neighbourhood. If people read, do they know what they read? What do they like to read best? Isn't it better to get to know a region first hand rather than just read about it?

17 c *A wise agreement* on the possible activities of people on earth. (With coloured felt-tip pens.) If life is to be preserved on our planet, humankind must come to its senses. In coloured blocks on the map you can see what people should agree on: blue blocks represent the protection of water in the oceans and rivers, of rain water and ground water. Green blocks show the protection of all plant and animal species. Yellow blocks represent the utilisation of solar energy. In other colours the children showed the need for education, the protection of cultural monuments and recycling of waste. 'And that black block?' we asked. 'That represents recognising our stupidity and stopping it before it is too late.'

17 c

Astrophysicists admit that our universe is perhaps only a little universe among other universes with other physical properties and space/time coordinates. If you discovered that the foam can be coloured and the bubbles placed on a piece of paper, you can get other, more permanent pictures. Don't hesitate to try to draw the Big Bang with a pencil, brush or mouse. Some of the pictures might provide inspiration (1, 2, 8, 9, 10 a, b, 11 a–c). Perhaps the most interesting is the constant growing and spreading of the space/time foam in picture 11, produced by older boys on the computer.

Naturally we all thought of looking at pictures of what is going on in our uni-

17 d

17 d *My trip around the world.* (Drawn with felt-tip pens on a map.) It is marvellous to really get to know the world; to experience it directly. How many well-known travellers and explorers do you know? Can you reach the North Pole by foot? Where are the as yet undiscovered regions? And now we shall land on the Galapagos Islands (at least on the map). I passed the island of Borneo which looks like a bear, but do bears actually live there? How many other connections can you think of when looking at drawing the travelling on the map? Let's hurry to the library and read about the places we found on the map. One of the younger boys followed the 'footsteps' of Jacques Cousteau on the map. He had watched all his documentaries on TV, then drew his journeys on the map.

25

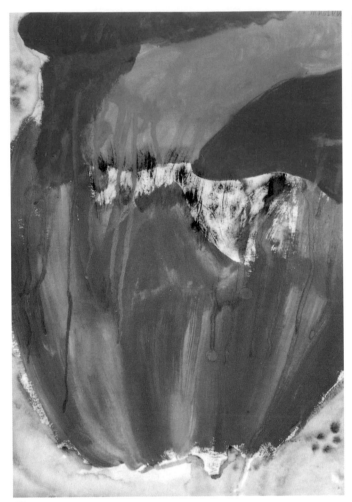

18 a   18 b

verse. It depends on you which popular science books you read. All of them have coloured illustrations of the spiral and ecliptic galaxies: these pictures are taken from radio maps prepared from radio-telescope observations. In all of them you will find planetary nebula, fascinating photographs of disturbances on the Sun. It is worthwhile copying them for the children and thus giving them the chance to complete their colourful fantasies. It is worth observing their own mini disturbances of red submerged in a wet area. A similar effect can be gained by modelling our own little planet with one volcano, three small oceans and mountains along the equator. Or does it actually look like a big nut? You can learn more from the pictures on pages 19 and 20.

It seems that stars are the silent witnesses of our walk around the universe, where we stand on tiptoe to see more at a greater distance. We do not see that we are standing on piles of our own rubbish, however, that we do not know what to do with. We wage small wars with people, the countryside and other animal species. Our home is the unique blue planet in the cold universe. What does it look like now and what will it look like in the future if we remain so engrossed in ourselves?

That is why we offer you a map; a new map of both the hemispheres or just the continents. We began by basing our considerations on pictures and

18 a, b *The stories of water and fire.* Children like to paint the elements. They are especially attracted to stories about volcanoes, so we looked at photocopies and talked about Vesuvius, which buried Pompeii in AD 79, about the island Krakatoa destroyed in 1883: about the thunder which could be heard 3,500 km away in Australia, and the thirty-metre-high waves which killed 36,000 people living as far away as Java. Do you know how hot lava is? (1,100 °C.) Do you know how the Devil's Tower, rising above Wyoming, was formed? (Lava rose very quickly and therefore cooled quickly, hardening into the marvellous tower.) We drew our stories of volcanoes, while some children tried to make models from paper then painted them and let the red colour run down their sides as if it was lava.

19 a　　　　　　　　　　　　　　　　　　　　　　　19 b

19 a, b *The children tried to create the eruption of a volcano* with the help of the KID-PIX program. At first, with the mouse, they drew a broad cupola (a peak volcano) with the dust, ash and gases spitting. Then they tried to complete the picture using colours. The red background recalls Krakatoa where the volcanic ash was blown by the wind and, for a whole year, made the world look as if it was always sundown. The last phase shows the island slowly sinking.

information about the origin of our planet, the shift of continents and the creation of oceans and dry land. We also used information about the cycles of Nature as shown on TV, and the campaigns of ecological movements. Older children can imagine events caused by the elements of fire, water, storms and wind of various intensities. Thanks to the computer some events, for example the eruption of a volcano, an earthquake or the eye of a hurricane can be traced from the calm beginnings up to the dramatic climax.

It is always beneficial for children if we use specific examples and materials. For the painting of water we have a cassette with the sound of a storm or the concert of roaring and rumbling thunder. When looking at pictures of Nature we can listen to the hum of the rainforest or the crackling of fire. The

20 *Crackling fire or eruptions on the Sun?* Either is possible, but how did this picture come about? It is actually very small (only 3.5 x 2.5 cm), but if you have a slide projector you can enlarge it on a white wall. We took a transparent foil, folded it and put it in the frame to protect the slide from both sides. We took a brush and put some thin colour between the foil; red and a little black. When we pressed the foil the colour spread, so when we projected our made-up slide we had large pictures of marvellous eruptions, colourful fireworks and dancing flames. You will find similar pictures on the following pages of our book. If you have a set of red flames in frames, you can project them in the dark accompanied by the sound of crackling fire on a tape. We bought some tapes with meditation music.

20

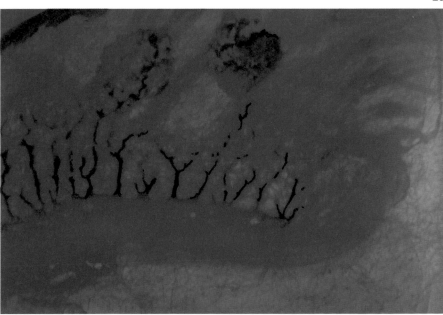

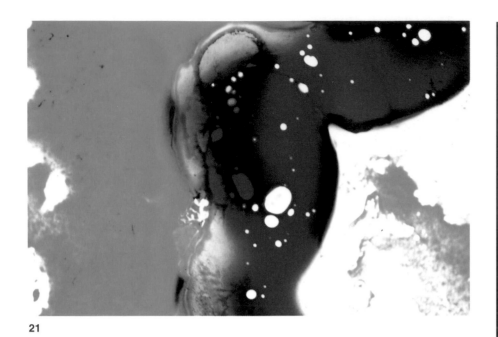

21

21 *The spirit of fire?* It appeared, to our surprise, when we projected a drop of thin red oil paint struggling with a drop of bluish water. Both were caught between the folded foil in the slide frame. You can let your imagination run wild while the spirit has its hands full as it struggles not to be overcome by the water. Enlarged on the wall to two metres, it looked frightening.

cassettes are available in shops, but let's try to do our own recording of a storm, a fire, water or a forest. For inspiration we can also use quite small things. We can put a few moldavites or pieces of lava from Etna or Vesuvius in our pocket. We can talk about the endlessness of time with a few pebbles in our palm or in front of a stalactite or some sand from the Sahara. I'm sure that friends will gladly bring you some of these things from their trips abroad. I received the feather of a Pacific gull in this way, and am completing my col-

22 a

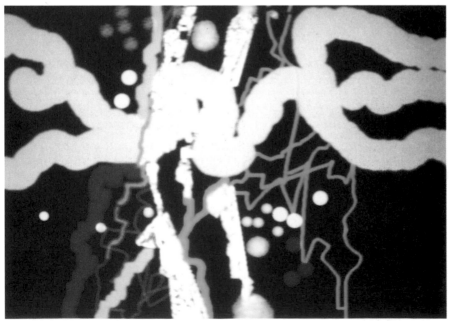

22 a–c *Lightning and thunder.* You can like or hate storms. You can see, hear and feel them. You may read many interesting things about them. On a picture shown in a film about Nature, we could see that at any given moment there are up to 1,800 storms occurring on earth. Pictures of lightning are fantastic. The sky first sends some introductory lightning and the earth replies, balancing the electrical tension. The lightning 'beats' from the earth up to the clouds; its temperature is about 15,000 degrees Centigrade. The heated air vibrates and we hear its bang or the more distant echo, as if waves of air were rolling across the earth. When painting pictures (b) and (c), but also the computer picture (a), we talked about our experiences of storms, then listened to a tape. Look how

28

22 b

22 c

the children drew the lightning; the clap itself, then the bang of the distant thunder. The sound spread on the computer drawing (a) like a horizontal din, but was like a bang on the two paintings (b, c).

lection of water from the oceans of the world and sand from the deserts. Some people have brought me amber from Poland, five large shells from Java and an amethyst crystal from Brazil. It all goes into a large box in which the children find what they want, then draw or paint it. Perhaps they don't yet realise that the box collection can again return to Nature. How? The boy with the moldavite in his hand, a stone from the universe, may later become an astrophysicist; the girl who dreams with a feather in her hand can become an ornithologist. How many future scientists, poets or painters can you find among those who are, for now, concealing their dreams in that box and in their childish pictures?

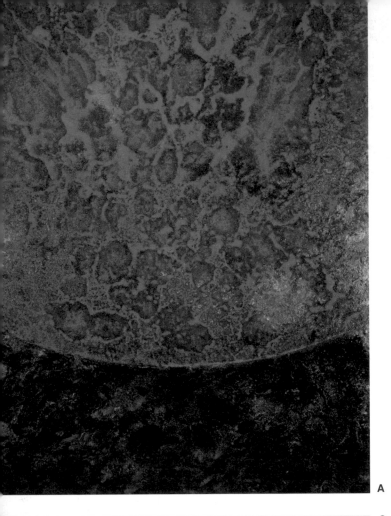

A

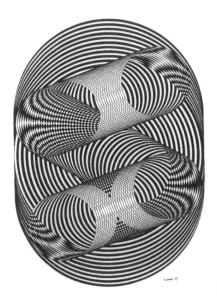

B

A   Kamil Linhart (born 1920), *Limited Composition No. 17*, 1989, combined technique, 113 x 85 cm. The sun can never squeeze into the picture of a single man. Only children paint the sun as a whole. The fate of all humankind is intertwined with its fate.

B   Vladislav Mirvald (born 1921), *Cylindrical Anti-perspective*, 1969, Indian ink on cardboard, 70 x 50 cm. What did the children say about this picture? 'We are walking through a cylinder, back and forth, we fall rapidly, time and space collide and we meet ourselves. The universe is like a toboggan. We float and – get off!'

C

D

C   Jiří Patera (born 1924), *Metronome*, 1994, oil on canvas, 95 x 80 cm. Every one of us thinks about our allotted time. We touch the universe. The hand of the metronome waves to the stars.

D   *Sundown*. Since ancient times, people have measured time by the rising and going down of the sun; each day it traces a vertical line of hope. It is good to remember this, just as our ancestors did.

E **Jiří Kornatovský** (born 1952), *Meditation*, 1993, charcoal drawing, 12 x 6 m. Meditation means reaching the truth through concentrated thought. It seems that birth and death are the only certainties...

F **Vladislav Mirvald** (born 1921), *Blotage with a lady's pen*, 1962, Indian ink on paper, 59 x 45 cm. What titles did the children make up? 'Me and my star. Me and my mummy. What I think about in the evening. My doll. A bone between the Big Bear and the Little Bear.'

G *How one looks at the stars*. A native of the Lesser Sunda Islands made several small statues during his lifetime. He and his descendants believe that after his death his soul will return to one of these statues, and they would keep it. The others would be sold at the market... I put it on the window sill so that it can see the stars.

Note: The four artists on these two pages as well as Zdenek Hůla (see page 54) are also important teachers. They taught many who also later became art teachers.

F

G

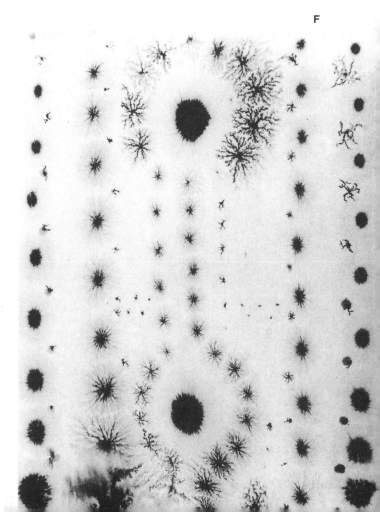

2

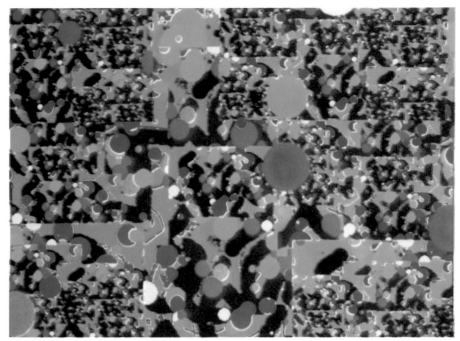

24

Creative Narrations about Plants

A maze of vegetation. Micro-events in plants. Conditions for plant communities. The art of talking to grass, a daffodil or a tree stump. The personification of Nature.

Close your eyes for a moment. I'll say the word 'plants'. What did you see? I tried it with the children and asked them to tell me quietly what they see in the flow of pictures appearing under their eyelids when they hear this word. At first it was a green, shapeless, moving colour, then it became lighter, as if they were in a forest. Somebody imagined a corner of their garden. Under their lids they saw fluttering leaves, various blossoms, rotating canopies of trees, as if they were lying under them in a wood. Some imagined they saw photos of the Amazon jungle as seen from a helicopter; clearly memories of a Nature film. Some children said that behind their closed eyes they saw the classroom windows with flowers and trees in front of the school. During the time that the eyes roamed behind the eyelids, the children took us to a botanical garden where they had seen exhibitions of blossoming cacti and orange trees. The huge leaf of Royal Victoria was suddenly replaced by a sea of orchids. Suddenly a boy interrupted the flow of descriptions of exotic flowers to tell us that he was eating spinach and had some tomatoes on his plate. Other children joined him and told me that they didn't like carrots, but do like fried cauliflower. By that time we were walking past a stand selling

23 *In the maze of vegetation* we find plants with varied leaves, shoots, flowers and fruits. The children painted them on a long strip of paper and every small artist 'talked' to their plant, not letting anyone threaten it. Every plant has its place, even though it might look as if confusion reigns. The plants talk to each other, lean on each other, touch each other and perhaps even dance together. The strip of paper with the plants was almost 10 metres long; too long for one photo. This picture comprises parts of the strip.

24 *The computer vegetation maze* was made from various graphic designs, lines, colours and a division of the whole area. Two older boys held a discussion over their computer screen and eventually agreed that the picture is like a mapping of plant species in a particular area, for example, in the rainforest. (See other phases on page 36.)

33

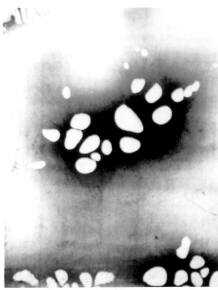

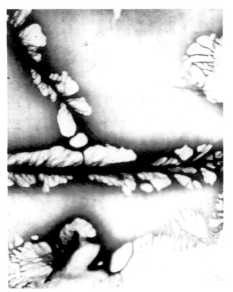

25 a   **25 b**

25 a, b *The glory of chlorophyll.*
In biology the children took their
first steps by becoming acquainted
with the essence of life and its origin.
They knew that most plants contain
green colour called chlorophyll, and
the plants 'produce' food by
photosynthesis. About 2.5 billion
years ago the plants learnt to bind
hydrogen with water (H_2O) and freed
oxygen. They produced so much that
they enabled all animals to breathe.
And besides that, all animals feed on
plants. Even though the first algae
and diatoms look somewhat different,
what we produced between two of our
small foils and projected on a white
wall looked very similar to the origin of
life on earth. All we had to do was put
a small drop of green between the
foils and then put it in a slide frame.

fruit and vegetables. Somebody then explained that he could hear the rust-
ling of bags with lime blossoms and nettles which his grandmother had dried.
Instead of being in a shop selling vegetables, we were suddenly in a phar-
macy, then a tea room, and even in a carpenter's shop where we walked on
sawdust. Somebody said 'coal' and so we went down not into a mine, but
into primeval times. The children knew the pictures of horsetails, club-moss
and lycopodium or fern from Zeman's film *A Trip to Primeval Times*. I suggested they close their eyes and look up, as those plants of 300 million years
ago were up to 20 metres high.

And then suddenly, without any apparent reason, the boy who had been

26

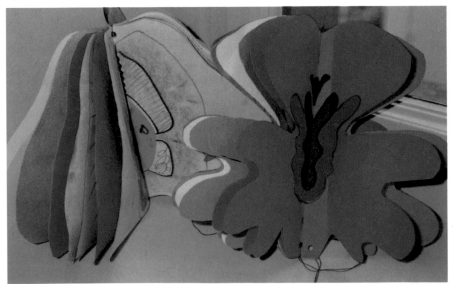

26 *We imagined the mystery
of the heredity of plant species* to be
like a book with many pages, which all
the little seeds read. The pages, in the
form of fruit, seeds, pips or nuts, have
a graphic symbol or specific
information about what the plant
must remember. For example, the
Crataegus oxyacantha will blossom
in May and June; the *Pyrus communis*
will have pear-shaped and round
fruits ... The information can be turned
into art, either according to the actual
parts of the plant, or according to
illustrations in an atlas. Which do
you prefer?

27 a

27 a–d *How do plants measure time?* By sprouting, growing, ripening and returning their seeds to the soil to repeat their image: the shape of the stalk or stem, the arrangement of the leaves, flowering and the shape of the fruit. We tried this repetition and growth in the form of a collage made of several different coloured papers. At first the children put one on top of the other and drew their plant on the piece of paper on top. They then cut all the layers of paper according to this drawing. By composing the coloured parts of the plant in separate stages, their plant started to grow. It seemed that the change of colour reflected the various stages of growth.

27 b

eating the spinach said, 'General Sherman!' Almost all of us opened our eyes in surprise. 'What's so surprising? The horsetails are dwarfs compared to this General. He measures 83 metres!' We quickly pulled out our *ABC of Nature*, and read: 'The most mighty of all living organisms are the sequoias, coniferous trees of great height. The record is at the moment held by the General Sherman in the National Sequoia Park in California. It is a giant of

27 c

28 a

28 a, b *Creative considerations about the biotype.* The biotype is a natural environment which provides the living conditions for certain plants and animals to thrive. An orchid, for example, belongs to the rainforest while 1,500 species of cacti live in the desert regions. It is much more complicated than that, however, and you will need the book by David Attenborough, *The Living Planet*, to help you understand it further. The author describes communities of plants and animals in the jungle, desert, northern forests and wide oceans in an interesting and absorbing way. The children can try, not only on the computer screen, to create colourful features of a certain region and place the graphic signs representing plant and animal communities in it.

28 a *The biotype in the rainforest.*

83 metres, the diameter of the trunk is 10 m, and it weighs approximately 1,385 tons.'

And so we tried to embrace the General. We held hands and the boy himself measured the diameter of 10 m by his steps. There was not enough room for the trunk in our classroom; the gym was a better place. We also learnt

28 b

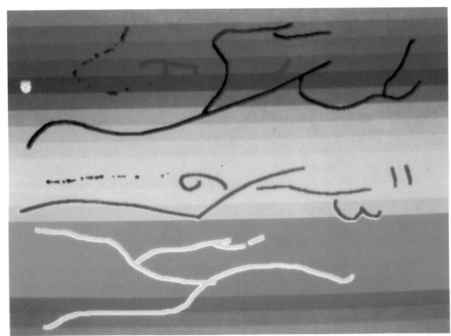

28 b *Various environments on the planet.* (Computer graphic presentation).

29 a *It's in the air!* You can feel it, even if you can't see it yet! Hurray! Spring is here. It gives you strength, energy and so much pleasure that you could fly. The spring wind chases the clouds, long hair and the branches of trees. It sings without words; just lalalala. Mummy, should I put on socks, a skirt or shorts? These discussions were held when working with the computer and the time went very quickly.

29 b *Spring leaves its marks.* The children thought of how it wakes the soil and tells the plant to get ready. It moves gently, careful not to crush any of the plants and avoids the puddles still covered with ice in the morning. Several children worked with the KID-PIX program, and many variations resulted from their discussions of springtime. You will find more on the following page.

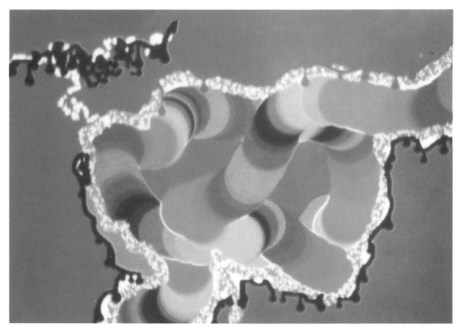

29 a

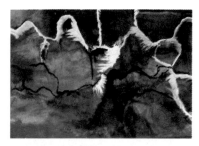

29 c

29 c *What does a living and a dead landscape look like?* This time the children drew on old maps. The living landscape is full of warmth and rivers looking like roots and branches. The dead countryside is burnt to dust or freezing cold.

from the book that the slimmer type, the evergreen sequoia, held the record at a height of 110 m. For that we had to measure our steps out in the street. When you are measuring by steps, you pass trees in your street. Do you know them? Wouldn't it be worthwhile to dividing the local trees among children; their patrons? They could, for example, write a mini-book about

29 b

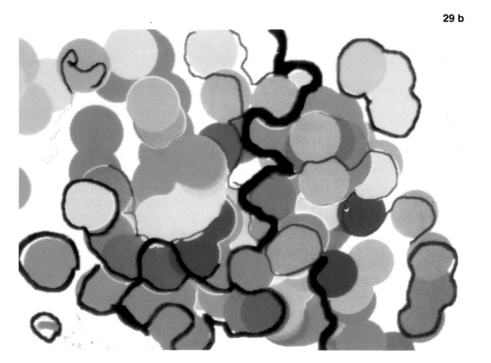

30a b
  c d

a maple in front of the school, collect its leaves in the various seasons, make rubbings of the bark and try to germinate its seeds. We have mentioned creative activities related to trees in the previous books, but here you will find further suggestions on pages 46–51.

If we go back to the above text about plants, we realise that the children mentioned only plants on land and they were attracted by the biggest, the trees. Biologists, however, know that plants evolved in the ancient seas. They took root on land, but many perished. The plant world currently consists of more than 350,000 species. What about looking at the smallest? The diatom, a microscopic unicellular alga, is one of the most numerous plants in the oceans. It has an interesting, almost geometrical shape. I'm sure the computer would like it. The children looked at their enlarged photocopies and tried to fill the computer screen with them (with the help of the KID-PIX program) as if they were looking into the ocean through a large magnifying glass in the window of a bathyscaphe .

Other children tried to enlarge the diatoms by painting them on as large a paper as possible and creating a huge drop representing the sea. In the same

30 a–d *How spring struggles with winter.* The author used the rubber stamps of trees from the computer program. They were placed in a kind of orchard still covered with snow, but with the ice beginning to break. Spring whizzed through the orchard in daytime (a), and is also there at night-time (b). The computer is able to produce a negative for night. There were other alternatives (c, d) and it was not at all clear which would win. Spring attacked winter and at once winter destroyed what spring had drawn. Spring then tried to dance winter to death in wild loops, but winter cut the loops. In the phasing of the seasonal metaphors, quick changes of the picture on screen are very popular with the children.

31 a, b *A coloured analysis of the feeling of spring.* The title sounds scientific, but it all came about without intention when playing the game of 'what will the computer make of the initial coloured drawing'. The children tried various graphic options and the computer brought the picture closer, divided it and cut it up. All this was done with the mouse, not the keyboard. Several children used the mouse. (In our second book, *Teaching Children to Paint,* a similar picture was made on a square net of a coloured analysis of the feeling of spring, but at that time the children worked with colours and brushes. It was a more artistic and demanding work but we should not criticise either. Both methods have their particular charm and fulfilled a purpose.)

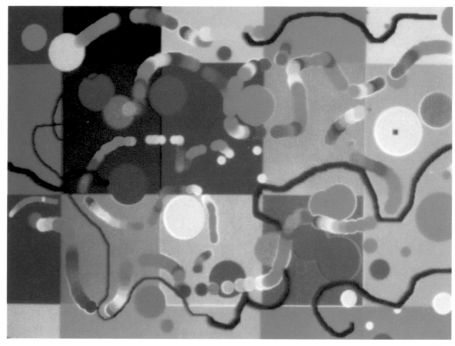

31 a

way it is possible to draw, with the help of a magnifying glass, a small piece of moss (polytrichum or sphagnum) which appears as a large 'forest'. Why not also try to enlarge the club-moss or ferns, creating a forest as it looked 345 million years ago?

31 b

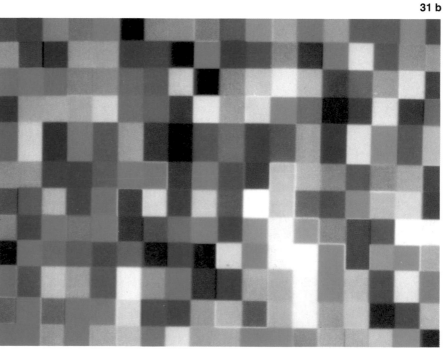

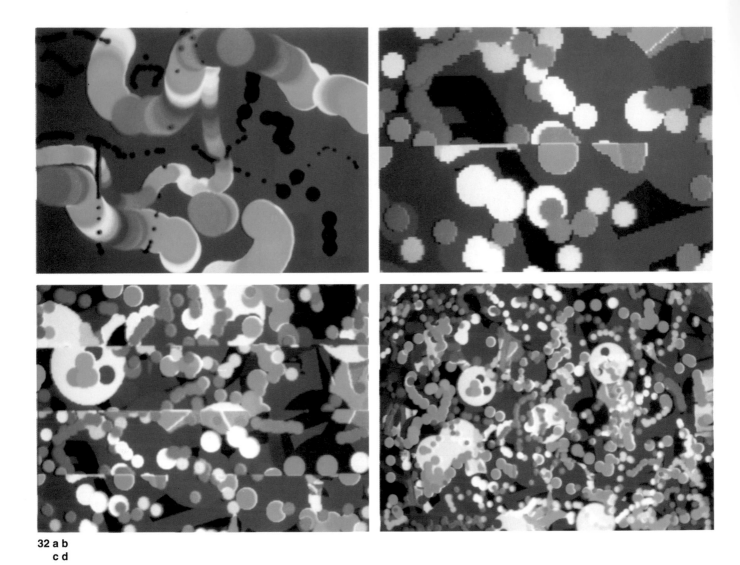

**32 a b
c d**

This is no forest, however. The present conifers or real seed plants were 'born' about 225 million years ago. The greatest discovery – the discovery of blossoming plants, trees, bushes, lianas, grass etcetera – was made 135 million years ago. Have we given you too many figures already?

Every plant needs its own surroundings. Let us show in stages on the computer what would happen to a cactus if we gave it water or fertilisers every day. What would happen to a hydrophilic plant if we put it in the sun without any water? Very few biotypes – either in the rainforest or a forest nearby, on a meadow or by a pond – can survive insensitive and harmful interference. This can be seen from the pictures on pages 36 and 37.

In the same way, children throughout the world have the cycles of Nature encoded within them. In moderate climates, childrens' pictures reflect the colours of Nature in the spring, summer, autumn and winter. In the previous books, which mapped the creative activities of children, we showed the seasons and months in paintings and more abstract forms of expression.

Computers made it possible for the children to test some of their ideas. Couples often took turns at the computer for ten minutes each. The children

32 a–d *How does spring turn into summer?* By adding warmth, variety and cheerfulness, by enlarging some parts of the picture and then cutting them up. There's nothing to it! We are playing because summer means holidays. On the screen we had such fireworks of colours and varieties that we were unable to take photos of all the stages and ideas. The children spoke about the holidays as a time full of adventure and experiences. Summer is the time of flying balls, happy gardens, colourful water, swimming suits and sunshades. Is your summer like this? We shall try to paint it on our desks.

33 a *How does autumn come?*
First, let us say, as yellow, orange and red little flames which jump from one tree to another, until the whole orchard looks as if it were on fire.

33 a

tried to change one season to another in several stages or by rapid 'phasing' of the original picture. They often used a picture of a park becoming green, then slowly yellow and red until it was finally bare and cold.

The colours of the sun and water then moved to the roots and settled for their winter sleep. From among the many experiments made with the

33 b

33 b *Autumn is also the windy time* when the children fly their kites. The two sides of autumn were created on the computer with the children using only the mouse. The ideas were so interesting that the children started to paint autumn orchards and kite flying. What stops us from walking through the heaps of coloured leaves and looking up through the colourful trees at the autumn sun?

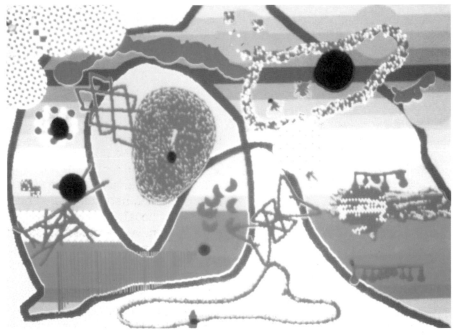

41

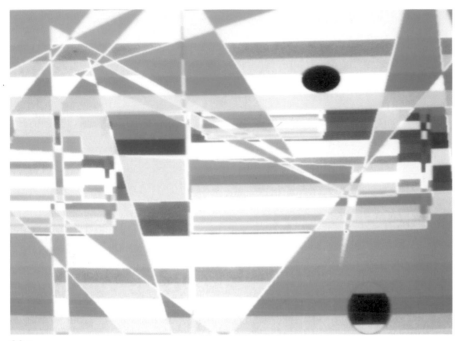

34 a

children using only the mouse, we show some examples on pages 38–42.
  In every season you can make one or more friends. Try to recall the greenery which you look at every day from your window. Would you be able to name some plant species framed in this space? You look at them throughout the year. Do you know how they change? What smell, colour or move-

34 b

34 a, b *What does winter look like?* It is a happy time for children if there is enough snow and the sun is shining.

Alternative **34 a** shows a skiing experience when everything moves so fast that even the colours blur. But then you have to slowly walk uphill when the ski-lift is out of order.

Alternative **34 b** illustrates a skating experience where the skates do not always do what their owner wants and we sometimes fall on our knees or nose.

Both pictures were quickly created on the computer using the graphic options.

34 c

34 c *Winter roses* were made by shaping crepe paper like snowballs to make a snowman. We miss flowers in the winter, so we made a bouquet from our paper roses and put it in the school corridor. You can also use the computer to add layers and build a snowman. What does a snowman look like in cross-section under an X-ray?

35 a, b *Autumn.* We need not paint autumn nor try it on the computer. We can study some quite small details. The children used small foils in slide frames to enlarge their 'miniatures' and project them on a wall.

35 a *Look out, this is not amber!* It's a drop of plum-jam between two foils. Plums are the titbits of autumn when everything ripens and sweetens.

35 b *This is what onion peel looks like* in autumn colours.

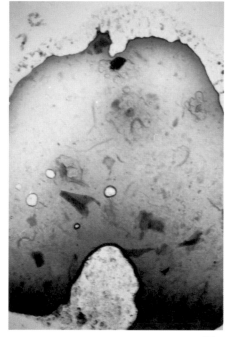

35 a   35 b

ments are typical for your plants in the spring, summer, autumn and winter? Which plant will become your friend this spring? It will be best if you chose one you can see from your window. It would be sad if you could not see at least some of our green friends.

36 a *Winter.* A leaf which the children carefully wrapped with a brush on a soft pad, looked like a whole tree when projected on the wall. It seems to be shivering with cold or sighing like a bare and discarded Christmas tree.

36 b *How did the children make frost for the window?* They crumpled a piece of old copying paper, pressed it on a foil, put it in a frame and projected it on the wall. We'd better not go out today: look at what is waiting for us in that big window. If we have several miniatures in framed foils, we can rearrange them or put them in cycles according to the material or mood. For example, I found a bird's feather in the garden during a spring walk, an alchemists' experience, illustrations for a poem about a dandelion ...

36 a   36 b

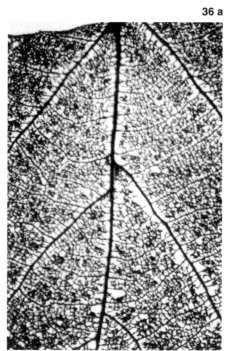

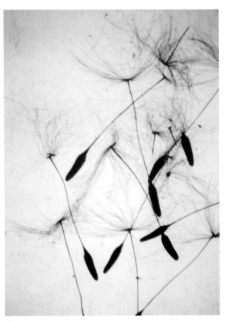

37 a

37 b

37 a–d   *A dandelion for all our senses.*

37 a, b   *Fine seeds* hanging under the sunshades can be blown away. We can count them and train our touch and vision. If we catch them and place them between a foil, we'll be surprised at how large they are when projected on a wall. The pictures differ according to how we arranged the fine seeds under the foil. Let's try to draw them with a pencil or computer mouse. Botanists will say that we are drawing samaras, finely articulated with long peaks and white fibres.

Just as societies are formed – and days of this or that are proclaimed as holidays – I suggested the children found a society of the friends of dandelions for an especially sunny spring. Why? It is the children's plant: it contains, even when we are grown-up, the memories of pure Nature both in and around our home town. We looked out of the window. They were everywhere where there was a bit of soil. Dandelions are the sun of children, trumpets,

37 c

37 d

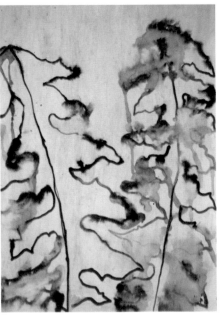

37 c, d   *What do you look like, dandelion?* We can draw you with a pencil or stick and Indian ink on dry or wet paper. We can see your folded, unfolded or faded blossoms. If we try to draw the leaves it will be interesting to read the various botanical terms which sound like curses: the leaves of the ground rose are like a crosscut saw shape, for example. Somewhere on our paper we can experiment with the colours of a dandelion. Take a piece of the leaf or blossom to determine the colour. What does the dandelion taste like? Can anyone get a recipe from their grandmother for dandelion salad or honey?

38 a–c *Dandelion stems* as trumpets and mysterious puzzles. First we held a concert with the help of narrow and wide dandelion stems. The thinner ones give a higher note while the wider are bass. Try to hold them in your palm in front of your mouth. By lifting your fingers you can regulate the height of the note. In the next silent phase, we put the stems in water and watched them turn into interesting spirals. We drew the most interesting ones with a pencil, but enlarged many times. Using these spirals, we created their spacial variations. We hung a dandelion spiral maze by a thread above our heads in the classroom. Some very wiggling ones were pinned to a board. Some children applied what they had learnt about the dandelion to the computer.

38 a

38 b

umbrellas, queens' crowns and honey for the sweet-tooth. Such a 'Dandelion Day' could provide even better ideas than those we offer in the captions under the pictures *A dandelion for all our senses* on pages 44 and 45. Together with the daisy, our dandelions taunt the gardener. They are considered a weed on the lawn or in the garden, something that should not be there, but the daisy doesn't mind. We can't imagine spring without it. If it is to be

38 c

39

39

39 *The bearded man.* This tree stump was all that remained of a huge plane-tree. It lived for a long time and every year more and more new shoots appeared; by autumn they were already one metre long. The park attendants cut them off but they reappeared in spring. It's alive! And so we animated the stump. The children gave it a face made of stones and twigs and sometimes they outlined the annual ring with coloured chalks. They made drawings of it and made up stories about it. Two children used the cut off twigs as brushes. Naturally they drew the 'bearded man' with a round face, dipping their twigs into Indian ink. Other children kept small plane-trees in flower pots.

our friend then we have to know more about it, as is always necessary for good friendship. It is important for children to know as much as possible about what they are drawing or painting. We give information concerning every drawing or painting.

The dandelion (*Taraxacum officinale*) belongs to the order of Aster or the family Aster, Compositae. It is a perennial plant with great regenerative abil-

40

40 *The story about the tree stump* could be created in various ways with the computer. A landscape with trees could originally be seen on the screen. The trees were black and snow was falling on them. Suddenly one could hear a call for help and a saw cut into one of the trees. A stump remained, but the annual rings continued to send their call for help into space. If you make a rubbing on soft paper of a stump in the forest, you can read from the rings what each of the years was like: whether it was damaged by arid years or even a fire. You can then put different colours on the respective rings and write about what the tree experienced that year next to each colour.

46

41 *Magic of a tree stump.* This is a stump of an acacia in our street. The tree had to give way to electrical lines. Occasionally I take two children to play with it. When the sun is shining we put life into it with the shadows of our hands. This creates the most bizarre bearded stump men, perhaps the sprite of the acacia tree, the shape of which we outline with chalk. They disappear after the first rain. They are sucked into the stump and so there is already a number of them. Let us try to find somebody who could explain to us and the children why a tree has to turn or has already turned into a stump.

41

ities. From a small portion of root it creates a new plant. We even counted the seeds from its blossom. We shall not give you the result so that you can discover it for yourselves. In the moderate climate of Europe and Asia it grows almost everywhere. What does it cure? Indigestion, liver diseases. It is like a tonic when you are tired or exhausted, and is a source of vitamins. It is excellent food for bees. It's worthwhile looking at them in the atlas

42

42 *Stump men?* Of course they exist, and not only in the form of Wild Men of the Woods and Fiery Men living in rotting phosphorescent stumps in the forest. They take care of little seedlings and chase away deer from the small trees so that their tops are not bitten off. I'm sure they often put a root in your way to stumble over when you make too much noise in the forest. It's good when the children make them come alive from stumps, branches, moss or cones found in the forest; try to find thirty stumps and bundles of twigs with cones for the thirty children in the class. On this and the following page you can see how the children tried to make a stump man from paper. They even used him as an actor.

43 a

43 b

of plants under the Aster. They are like stars sprinkled and shining on the meadows.

You can have armfuls of plants like the dandelion, and can lie down among them in the grass. People should not behave like extravagant consumers, however, even in the midst of such abundance. Humankind did not create a dandelion or a blade of grass and never will. To learn as much as possible about plants and to have contact with them is a person's vital duty, not only their pleasure.

We considered which summer plants we would form lasting friendships with. We could choose from chamomile, the willowherb or all kinds of grass. Chamomile can be perceived by all the senses: it strokes our legs along the path we walked in summer and it smells good in a cup of tea. Drawing it with fine strokes so as not to lose its character wasn't easy with a pencil or brush. It was even more difficult with the mouse.

Do you know the willowherb? We became interested in it because it is a rascal just like the dandelion. Its spikes with purple blossoms reach almost to your waist in every clearing, and it is also the first living thing to appear among the tree stumps after a forest fire. It lives in the area surrounding volcano

43 a–e *Stump men introduce themselves.* They are all the good spirits of trees. They will tell you the stories of an oak, pine, larch, or birch. How did they come about? Every child got a large piece of brown paper which they rolled up to form a cylinder or truncated cone. He was sad and didn't speak. With the help of coloured paper, the children were supposed to make him come alive. They cut some parts of the coloured body twice, often from a paper folded over. Sometimes they gave the stump man the shape of their fingers, and considered wings and camouflaging with leaves on their caps. The heads, made of coiled cones, nodded on the bodies. The children found inspiration for some of the leaves in the atlas. And their names? We discussed each figure ...

43 c

43 d

43 e

For example: (a) Larch Paw, (b) Strict Oak, (c) Tasselled Willow, (d) Dashing Thicket, (e) Bearded Blackthorne.

eruptions, and is first to grow in devastated countryside after a war. We found the volcano Mount St Helen on the map of North America, where the willow-herb is at home (the Americans call it fire-weed). In Great Britain the willow-herb is the most frequent, freely growing plant in towns and cities, and we have also waved to it not only from our window in Prague, but also from our cottage. It accompanied us all the way there. We drew it several times. Its hairy seeds are a surprising shape among the foils if we project them, en-larged, on a wall. If we want to introduce it to the computer, why not try to represent its feat of establishing itself and regenerating the vicinity of a vol-cano after an eruption? Is the unmistakable purple colour of the blossoms available in your graphics program?

What would summer be like without grass!? A meadow is a jungle of plant families that give pleasure to your body and soul. What do people keeping their lawn tidy with a mower know about mountain meadows that used to be cut with a scythe, but only after the farmer had waited for all the plants to stop blossoming? The construction of the blade of a narrow leaf of grass with its growing zone close to the earth is a small miracle, as is the formation of a root cluster.

49

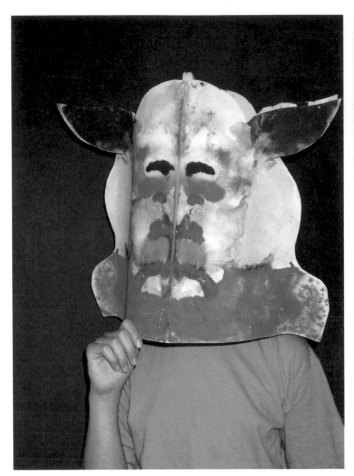

44 a

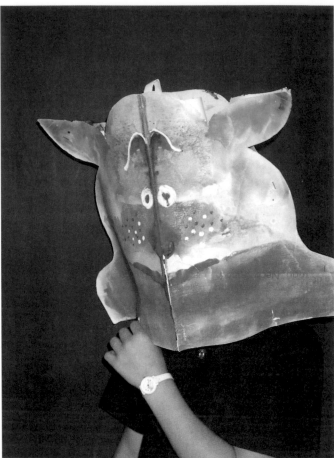

44 b

That is why grass can put up not only with droughts, but also survives a fire and regular cutting and sensible grazing. It heals wounds inflicted on Nature by humankind. Its family has roughly ten thousand species in the world, and it does not need insects for pollination; the wind moving its blades is enough. It is food for lizards and was created only 25 million years ago. If we put all dry land into one single circle, one quarter would be covered with grass. And so we sat down at the edge of the meadow, opened the atlas and looked for our friends the poa. I could hear greetings: 'Good morning, I am Fescue Grass!' – 'Hello, my name is Darnel.'

Can we recognise grass species according to their flowering when touching them with closed eyes? Can we draw a tuft of grass, making it more than a tangle of unclear lines in a confusing scribble? How should we differentiate the roots, blades and stems? How do we create the feeling of grass with the help of vertical illuminated lines offered by the computer? Could we enlarge on the computer cultivated grass: some corn perhaps? How can we best express the difference between the form of an ear of wheat, rye, barley or oats? Let the computer try. How can it meet a blade of grass? Can you show the stages: how a grain of wheat turns into a field, is harvested, ground into flour and made into a cake?

Our friendship with plants in the autumn is happy and sweet, but I know

44 a, b *Guardians of the forest?* The children changed into these fantastic creatures. They made them with diluted colours in monotype, printing the colours according to their axis. Every head has two sides. Can you recognise the guardian who ensures that no fire breaks out in the forest? It's the one with the red face. The one with the blue beard makes sure that there is enough moisture in the forest pools and brooks for the wild animals to drink.

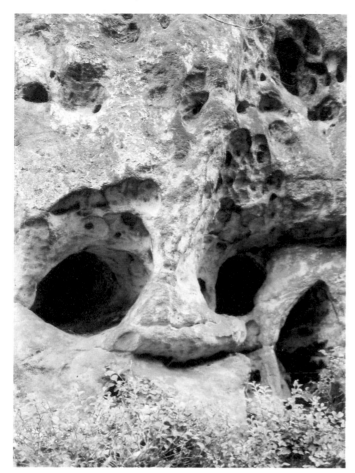

45

46

45 *Eyes?* There's no doubt that someone is watching you in the forest. The rocks have seen many generations of trees. We found this rock on a trip to Hřensko in north-west Bohemia. The most varied details can be touched and drawn with rubbings made of them. We put two white stones into two hollows so that the eyes could see. Try to draw the enlarged face of a rock giant according to this picture.

46 *The chestnut feast.* Swings used to hang on this chestnut tree for three generations. Three generations of children played with its leaves and little chestnuts, therefore it deserves a holiday. We made a wreath and a necklace of its fruit and stuck the faces of three generations to its rind, shaped from soft aluminium according to our own faces. In the picture you can see the youngest face.

children who have never picked themselves an apple or a plum from a tree. For children in towns, autumn is connected to trees in the streets and parks. I do not know a child who has never picked up a red maple leaf or does not collect chestnuts in their pocket. We tried to find our trees both in the town and in fairytales, myths and legends. Autumn pleasures connected to trees are numerous in the creative arts and their personification is given on the last pages of this chapter. You will meet not only the stump men, the guardians of the forest, but can also experience the Chestnut Holiday. In the following text we would like to recommend a small creative series on the subject, What turned a girl into a tree? Autumn, it seems, is also a magician. The children tried to take down its various magic formulas derived from drawings of branches without leaves, rubbings of bark and prints of leaves.

What is the writing of a tree? The children used it not only for the magic formulas, but also on the monitor tracing a twig placed on the screen. They tried to turn their hands, eyes and legs into a tree. They drew prolonged branches and twisted roots following their spread fingers. The tree looked through the eyes of knots. They also based their drawings on ballads. In one a woman turned into a willow; in another a girl became a maple. In a fairy-tale a girl hid from danger in a lime tree, while a curse changed a princess into a poplar. How can human life be linked to a tree? Very firmly:

47 a–c *Branches and roots.*
Don't you sometimes feel as if you were a tree? Let's try to imagine that we are trees. We raise our arms and close our eyes. Now the wind is blowing through our branches; it becomes stronger and we have to resist it all we can. How does a birch move in the wind? And how an oak, willow, aspen or larch? We cut out our hands (branches) from coloured paper and attached them to the image of a human tree. The idea that our tree should also have roots came later. When we asked the children what tree they would like to be, they agreed on a strong oak, a lime-tree, which everyone loves, and an apple tree which has lovely blossoms. Nobody, however, wanted to be a Christmas tree.

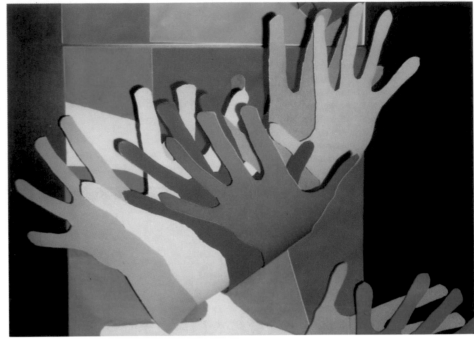

47 a b c

If a person cuts down one hectare of rainforest, they destroy 100 species of trees. The Native Americans say that even dead forests take their revenge. How? It is the large forests that supply the world with one fifth of the oxygen needed. We often hear about the green lungs of the planet, but still do everything possible to stop the breathing.

One tree alone, the last of its kind, can save humankind if its secret is discovered. In the northern part of Borneo the Calophyllum tree has perished, although research had shown that its extract could stop the HIV virus. Is there any hope? This tree was thought extinct, but was found at last outside Borneo in a botanical garden in Singapore. (I read about this in a newspaper in 1996.)

It is sometimes sad to take care of trees. We put a fence around trees and keep them in a reserve and then we wonder what an oak feels like, which decided to grow a few feet beyond the fence.

48 *We discovered the branch-hand in a park* not far away from our school. The children had to stretch up to see that the hand had not been pushed into the tree. Two little children were willing to believe that an enchanted creature lived there; they know about them from fairytales. Or did the tree perhaps want to shake their hands?

48

All too late we try to punish the self-appointed wood cutters with fines – people who objected to a hundred-year-old tree throwing a shadow at their window, or those who insisted on leading the electric current through an alley or a park. As desperate foresters we cut the branches of small conifers to make them look so ugly that no thief of Christmas trees would want them. Let us try to anticipate so as not to come too late to trees that are already dead or of which only stumps are left.

A

B

C

A **Zdenek Hůla** (born 1948), *Currents,* 1992, wooden ceiling in the belfry of the Church of St. John the Baptist in Kostelec nad Černými lesy, 525 x 400 cm. The sculptor drew the swinging sound of a bell like waving branches in the wind. What are the roofs and ceilings of people's houses comprised of? 'The gestures of trees make drawings in the town square,' is how the artist explained another one of his creations.

B–D **Čestmír Suška** (born 1952).

B *The Great Messenger,* a poplar on the Kampa, 1995–6, 500 cm (detail of the crown). I walked by this poplar as a little girl with my grandmother, then with my son and, ten years ago, with my grandson. I didn't presume that the tree would again give me its message of time in the form of a monumental sculpture in an exhibition space.

C *Once more the Great Messenger* — this time its trunk. Does anyone live in it? No, only the visitors to the exhibition look at each other in surprise, impressed by the monumental strength and spiritual message of the tree and the sculpture.

D

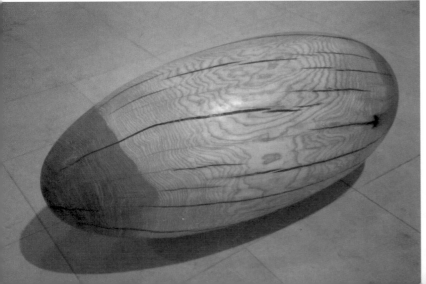

D *A pip*, wooden sculpture, 1996, 140 cm. If such a big poplar grew from a small seed (B, C), how big would a tree be that grew from this pip? Or let's look at it another way. Imagine that you are an ant ... How big would a hazelnut be in relation to you?

E *Wild vine on the Kampa Island* is vainly struggling with the shoots of graffiti. Perhaps we are surprised by the contrast between the anonymous, futile aggression and the modesty of the golden vegetation whose existence we endanger.

F *The doors to the trees are closed.* In the evenings and early mornings they open and we can hear squeaking, laughter and other noises around the tree. The children can draw or paint those who live in the tree.

E

G *A blade of grass.* It is sufficient to take a thimble of soil and a drop of rain. With its green colour it greatly differs from the red car, the railing and the spilt varnish. An island of softness struggles with the hardness of asphalt. I should like to save it and take it to a meadow. I didn't do it, but I shall send its picture to the world.

F

G

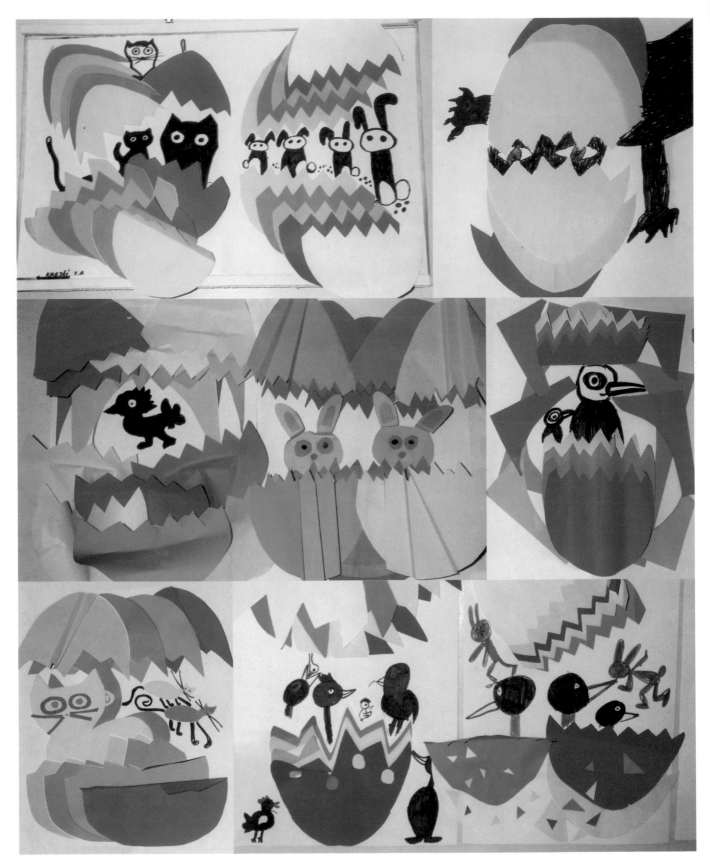

3

50

Creative Talks with Animals

What pecks out of an egg? Reading from footprints. About the movement and communication among animals. Stories about butterflies, fish and birds. Myths and fairytale performances.

When looking at the stars one's head often spins. Something similar can happen to you if you are lucky enough to hold a warm egg in your hand and can see the chick's beak through a small hole it pecked open. Our hen gave me this unforgettable experience when I was six years old. If you don't have such a friendly mother hen, however, do not try this.

The subject of the egg can be repeated with the children using a variety of methods and materials. We shall include suggestions other than the two examples on these pages. It's possible to show how a pullet is formed in an egg and how it hatches – a chicken, ostrich, duck or a fantastic household god – using phasing on the computer. It's a good idea to have a look at a Nature-study book, and see what traits, inherited from its parents, this new creature already has in the shell. Don't forget that it's tightly packed inside its shell; it doesn't float before it pecks its way out.

As another alternative, we could try to illustrate old legends to understand how important the egg was for early civilisations trying to understand how the world was created. The Finnish legend about the origin of the world has several different stages that could be painted. A teal allegedly laid several eggs into the lap of the Mother Water, the goddess of creation. She knew nothing

49 *What pecked out of an egg?* Making collages of coloured paper, the children played with the idea of spring, birth and the customs related to Easter. By arranging the paper in layers from which the children cut out the eggs, the pictures flickered merrily, vibrating as if something was hatching out of a shell. The little black creatures could be seen in their various coloured shells. Some children suggested that they were actually happy black goblins or chicken from fairytales who only help those who deserve it. They peck anyone who wants to have everything for themselves.

50 *The spiral of time.* An egg is actually a small miracle. The yolk of a bird's egg is one huge cell, the core of the future creature. We looked at pictures of various birds, their eggs and nests. The children then drew what could not be seen on to the eggs themselves. The nest around the shells was a magic line, spiral or circle, which indicated repetition, protection against danger, an infinite cycle...

57

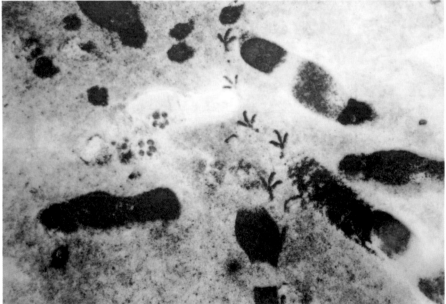

51 a b

51 a, b *Where do various times meet?* In the picture we see the crossing footprints of people and other people, people and birds, a bird and a cat, a cat and a person. The footprints you see in the wet snow were certainly not made at the same time. Let's imagine, however, that they were. What did the person have to say to the crow, pigeon or cat? Can you tell which animal the children made from the footprints in the snow? A cat! It looks as if someone carried it and put it down on its hind legs only. It did not want to go down into the snow, however, so the person picked it up again and hid it under their coat. We tried it on paper in the classroom. The children 'walked' on the paper with the help of stamps cut out of potatoes and stencils of their own hands. Are we poultry or waterfowl, are we mice, foxes or hares?

better than to let them roll away and they broke. The shell fragments turned into the sun, the earth, the moon and the sky and clouds.

The god of love, Eros, who was hatched from a silver egg by the goddess of the night, Nyx, did something similar with the shell according to an ancient Greek legend. In this version Eros's father was the wind and his son created a new space for him from the shell of his egg; the earth and the sky. The people of the Samoan Islands believe that their heavenly god was hatched and created their islands for them.

If you have a brush, pencil or mouse handy, try to illustrate these legends. There are many about the differences in nests and birds' eggs. You can gain the strongest impressions, however, from chance encounters. Do you know

52 *Footprints of people and animals* take different paths, but they often walk together. You can see animal prints made before humankind existed. Can children imagine the footprints of extinct dinosaurs? They walked along a 20-metre-long strip of paper and you can see the result in the photo. The children were tireless, describing what the animal looked like, how much it weighed, whether it was running or crawling, all according to the footprints. They found some pictures of petrified prints of dinosaurs and were pleased when they found that they had made up similar ones themselves. The strip of paper with the footprints hung from the third floor down to the ground floor, so the imaginary creatures walked through the whole school.

52

if there is a nest anywhere in your area? Do you know who lives in it? Do those inhabitants sing? Try to write down their song.

There are many subjects like the egg that disrupt the orderly arrangement of the zoology textbooks that classify the animal world from the most primitive creatures up to mammals. We shall do this with the blessing of such significant natural scientists as David Attenborough and Gerald Durrell.

Let's now look at some other subjects: the footprints of animals; how animals move; the methods of communication; how animals disguise themselves; what tools they use; their sounds and signals; how animals see and hear; how they migrate; what and how people can learn from animals. Can you think of anything else? Not every subject immediately offers ideas for

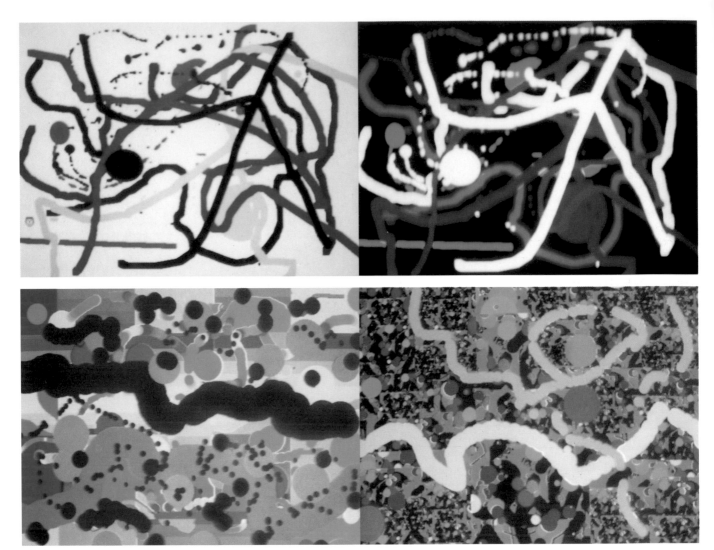

53 a b
54 a b

creative activities; they have to be looked for. If the children only watch and gain strong impressions, do not forget that perception is also creation.

The subject of animal footprints made us realise how different encounters with and movements of animals can be. On the computer screen a mouse can run about, leave footprints behind and then hide from the cat in a hole. Much more interesting, however, were footprints on a long strip of paper, where the children were able to become part of 'their' animal, whether walking, running, jumping or crawling. It might be of interest to know that the children also made up a 'language' for their animal. It was no ordinary miaowing or quacking, hissing or chirping. For inspiration we used a tape with sounds from the awakening jungle.

For the next subject where we decided to study the movement of animals, we first had to see how we ourselves move. We touched our legs and arms with great concentration. 'It's certainly the muscles that make us move,' said some boys as they contracted their muscles. 'No, movement is caused by the bones to which the muscles are attached by tendons,' and the girls per-

53 a, b *The leg of a bird in motion.* (Positive and negative of the computer graphics.) Have you heard or seen a rooster when he calls the hen to pick some grains he has found? A clucking hen calls more gently. We tried to record our creations on the computer. The children drew the frenzied scratching movements and what the rooster found: grain and earthworms.

54 a, b *The paths of earthworms.* Let's imagine what is going on underground. Tunnel-like passages are full of surprises and discoveries. We drew a kind of mining not only with a pencil or pen, but also with the computer mouse.

55 a *What the little octopus tells the sailors.* This is actually an illustration of a made-up 'sea tale'. The octopus was drawn by outlining a child's hand, the prolonged fingers turning into five tentacles. With their wavy dance they tell the sailors what dangers they might encounter at sea. They can even practise magic. The brown leads the ship to the treasure island, the blue calms the ocean storm, the green tells the sailors which fish they can catch. And the red? That will take the ship safely to its home port. The children also learnt how big the octopuses can become with a huge one, including its tentacles, measuring up to 20 metres and weighing more than one ton. (Do you know that the Australian dry-land earthworm, which is also an invertebrate, measures 3 metres? Czech fishermen would probably run away from it.)

55 a

formed a kind of ballet about the flight of a swan. It's true that the muscles must be supported by something. For mammals it is the skeleton, but there is also the conch of the lamellibranch and the snail shell. I open a small terrarium, where a couple of snails, a rainworm and a caterpillar gravely crawl over a piece of lettuce. Each one moves very differently. We describe their movements. What should the children draw? Lettuce and some snails and, under the leaves, the meetings of rainworms and caterpillars. Whether their

55 b

55 b *Some children could also try the dance of the octopus* on the computer.

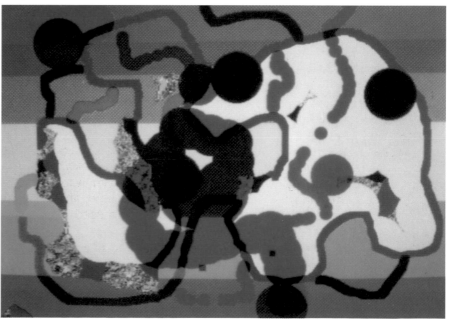

56 a

56 a, b *The handwriting of butterflies.* Don't you think that the butterfly opens its wings like the pages of a book? Let's find out what it is trying to tell us: 'I have scales on my wings and thanks to them my wings are colourful. I am able to use them for camouflage. The biggest of us is the Alexandrina from New Guinea. Its wings measure 30 cm. In South America there are 6,000 species of us, in North America 700 species, and in Europe only 400 species. We can migrate like birds. A hundred million North American monarchs fly south. The children drew me with chalk powder on wet paper. They used Indian ink to put the butterfly handwriting on my wings. It tells of what we like to eat, how we become larvae and how we make silk. A letter was also written in butterfly handwriting (b). Once I wrote it in the rain and another time I wrote it when it was hot. I sent it to my brother in the Himalayas, where he lives 6,000 m above sea level.'

56 b

prints are visible on the leaf or not, it would be interesting to put them on paper. Some children want to map the paths of the snails on the computer.

Documentation about the movement of animals should be classified and presented systematically on panels or boards. Children like to bring pictures from books and calendars, and thus a flying eagle meets an albatross while next to them we see a fluttering hummingbird, a graceful jumping dolphin beside a cheetah or horse running at full speed. During other lessons you could illustrate with a real feather the long-standing desire of humankind to be able to fly – Icarus and Pegasus.

Inspiration for the 'migration of animals' subject can be found in many books, but the most attractive option was the chance to participate in the 'African Odyssey' project organised by Czech ornithologists. The travels of stork

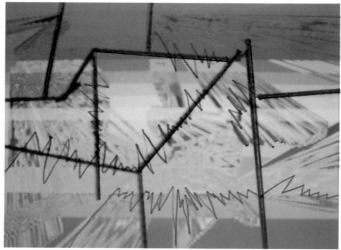

57 a   **57 b**

57 a–c   *What butterflies flew out of the computer?* Unbelievably colourful ones, of course. The children tried several variations on the life of a butterfly:

57 a   *How they fly* over a colourful meadow and get lost in it.

57 b   *How moths flap their wings* and suddenly drop vertically to avoid the insectivorous bats.

57 c   *How they recognise blossoms* according to their colour and smell.

illustrate that bonds between scientists, teachers and children are meaningful if they link the scientific importance of the subject with the children's imagination and their desire to uncover secrets. Storks have 'one leg in Bohemia and one leg in Africa'. Our story concerns the protected black stork (*Ciconia nigra*) which is more fearful than the white stork, and builds its nest on trees or rocks. About 350 pairs live in Bohemia, but in Africa where it spends the winter there are only 10 pairs confirmed. (There are a thousand times more white storks.) And so the ornithologists decided on the African Odyssey pro-

57 c

58 a

58 a–e *Communication: the fights and reconciliations* of fur and feather creatures on these two pages are more a reflection of people than animals. They were drawn by older children working in couples on large pieces of paper. First the children agreed on the situation in which their creatures were to appear. The children put their hands on the paper to outline the gestures and the basic scene. They then used Indian ink and bundles of 3–5 wooden sticks so that they could draw the structure of the feathers or fur more quickly. At the end the children discussed what text should be added to the pictures:

58 a *'A small but courageous creature* dared to attack the ruler of the clouds. The bird can't fly because its wings are too large. It must defend itself against the wild creature.'

ject, inviting the children to join. First we read books about the migration of birds, drew their routes on maps, painted storks' nests complete with young and parents, and their environment. Our storks were given the names Kristyne and Susan. The ornithologists put a small knapsack on their backs containing a satellite transmitter which told them where the storks were at any given moment. According to the news on TV or radio, the children could draw what their storks saw, where they were and what they were doing. Susan had had her transmitter knapsack since the autumn of 1995, and the ornitholo-

58 b

58 b *'Let me be, I give up.* It is not worth fighting over.'

58 c

58 d

58 c *'We are not fighting,* just fencing using all our limbs and exchanging our opinions loudly.'

58 d *'See what we have come to!* It's lucky we didn't hurt each other more. Both of us are surprised.'

gists joined her in Africa some time later. On TV we could watch 'our Susan' and the ornithologists finding their way in the African bush. On 28 January 1997, however, the children heard that a pile of feathers and the knapsack with the transmitter were all that was left of this rare bird. Somebody had killed her, probably with a stone: pure vandalism. She died near the village of Seged in Ethiopia. The results obtained by the expedition will be handed over to the Ethiopian authorities and protectors of Nature. Susan's knapsack and transmitter are now carried by another stork, a male called Adis which is flying from Africa to the Czech Republic. Kristyne returned to Bohemia at the beginning of April 1997. Perhaps she was able to repair her nest which was damaged by a storm in the winter. (Unfortunately Moravia lost many storks during floods in summer 1997.) We dedicated our bird pictures to the stork Susan. Some of them are on pages 68 and 69. The children painted

58 e *'Listen, you funny furry ball,* I want to box according to the rules but instead you are tickling me. I'd better leave you alone. You are a strange creature who I don't understand.'

58 e

59 a

59 a–e *Communication: the creative expression of intimacy,* friendship, petting and animal play were again an opportunity for the twelve-year-old children to draw, in a roundabout way, what is going on between people. The method was the same as on the previous page, but there it was more like solving a conflict situation of fights and quarrels. After their friendly contact was over they made their furry creatures come alive, talking for them and explaining the kind of communication they had in mind. The children again worked in pairs.

59 a *'We are queer creatures,* perhaps the last of our kind on this earth. Why we stick close together: it makes us feel good and we must protect each other. What are we called? Let's say Roundies or Fluffies. What names will you give us?'

Susan as a 'rainbow aviator' or white messenger. And why on the computer? Didn't the ornithologists also use clever equipment for their research?

The migration subject was also connected with movement, but this time of butterflies. Children like to draw and paint them and even on the computer it is possible to create the symmetrical shapes suitable for butterflies. We tried to find the interesting aspects of a butterfly's life. The children were surprised that the well-known cabbage butterfly flies up to 300 kilometres during its short life of 3–4 weeks, and the North American monarchs fascinated them.

59 b

59 b *'I want to play with you, do you hear?* See how good activity is for me and what a lithe cat I am. You just lie about getting fat and it has turned you into a shaggy melon. Get moving!'

59 c *'Tomcats are the laziest creatures* under the sun, and this one is their boss ... You see, my little master, I am guarding you and I have nothing in common with this lazybones. How can you pat it?'

59 c

59 e *'Don't be afraid, puppy!* Do I always have to push you? We shall watch together; you shall become a watchdog when you grow up.'

59 e

Did you see the picture of millions of monarchs which, after their 3,000-kilo-metre-long trip from Canada to Mexico, sit on the same trees as their fore-bears did? If every child cuts out and draws at least three monarchs, the school can admire its 'tree' on which the paper monarchs sit. Wouldn't you also like to make such a tree?

While our heads were full of butterflies, a mystery occurred: hummingbirds were allegedly flying around the flower stands on the square! There were many theories about where they had come from. Perhaps they had arrived

59 d

59 d *'All babies cause trouble,* including kittens. They turned me into a mobile bed, a slide, hide-and-seek. They test their claws on me. I am still on guard, and if you try to touch and hurt them I will come at you like a rocket. At the moment I am just carefully watching you.'

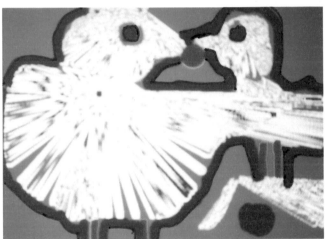

60 a   **60 b c**

with the exotic flowers. Somebody insisted that this little jewel with its fat body and longish beak was not a hummingbird but a butterfly. Our search continued, but we needed some professional help from the butterfly atlas and the department of entomology at the museum. We chose two butterfly candidates: we decided the exotic *Hotinus pyrorhynchus* had been packed by mistake with the flowers on far-away Borneo. The second butterfly candidate was the correct one, as determined by an entomologist. It was not a hummingbird or a cicada, but a *Macroglossa stellatarum*. He described it in such an interesting way that we looked in the atlas, drew it and read about its relatives the hawkmoth. Its Latin name sounds exotic, like a magic formula (*Macroglossa stellatarum*) and it still flies in the squares in Prague. Our pictures on pages 62 and 63 are devoted to it.

More impressive than the travelling of fragile butterflies is the migration of whales. We found the coast of Siberia, the Bering Strait on the map, and drew the route of the balaena gray whale over to the Gulf of Mexico. Hosts of people wait for the Moby Dick Parade off the coast of Southern California. They could set their watches by them; the whales always pass through the Bering Strait at the same time.

This time the children did not only deal with the migration of whales, but

60 a–c   *How birds love their young ones.* They not only build a nest, lay eggs, warm them with their own bodies and turn them over. They also feed the hatchlings, teach them to fly and look for food. They also know how to protect their young. The loons carry their chicks on their backs, as if on the deck of a ship. They even dive with them. The screech owl is not the only one to distract its enemies by pretending to have hurt its wing. Every bird species behaves differently as a parent. The children drew 'feeding', which reminds them of kisses. First they tried to paint it (a), then they also used the computer (b, c).

61 a

61 b

61 a *The bird house is empty.*
'The March Family' used to live there.
The little children regarded the birds'
house as a real home. It can be taken
apart. Not every bird's house suits
every bird species.

61 b *Do you know how much
energy migrating birds consume?*
The boy who drew this picture of
a bird said that it is 'full of energy'.
People are carried in a plane, but
a bird flies alone. Following interesting
information from books describing
the gathering and migration of birds,
we found the paths on the globe flown
by the black storks when they leave
the Czech Republic. We were also
interested in the path of the swallows.
They fly 11,000 km from Norway to
South America. The blue-winged teal
flies 10,000 km from the North
American prairies to Argentina. The
long-beaked tern flies twice a year
from pole to pole: 30,000 km.

61 c *The gathering of birds* was
painted by two girls from the second
class. On the right side of the picture
are so many birds that you cannot see
the sky, but the birds are not of
a particular species. The picture was
painted at the same time that we read
about the death of the black stork
Zuzana (Susan) in Ethiopia, which the
children had been following according
to news supplied by ornithologists.

were also given a sound puzzle. Who is playing this queer instrument? Does
it speak or sing? We were listening to the most talkative of all the cetaceans
– the keporkaky. At the end of their concert we read the interesting book *The
Whale – the Ruler of the Sea* by Jacques Cousteau and Philippe Diolé. We
then listened again to the concert and the children began to draw. You can
find their pictures on page 70.

When talking about butterflies we tried to interpret their flight by line and
colour and imagine this as some kind of message written in 'butterfly writing'

61 c

62 a

62 b

62 a–d *How do hundred-ton giants sing?* Knocking, whistling and sighing can be heard from the dark depths of the ocean. We listened to the songs of whales on a tape and drew pictures. Some children created a 'whale score' according to the sounds, while others created 'a dance of giant bodies'. Some drew a seascape; the mood which the sounds evoked. You can learn many interesting things from the book *The Whale — the Ruler of the Sea*, by Jacques Cousteau and Philippe Diolé. Can you guess who the only enemy of whales is?

in the air or a colourful meadow. That was another step in the direction of finding out whether animals communicate with each other and whether they could perhaps talk to us. Would we be able to draw or paint this?

Whether the animals are quarrelling, fight, protecting or being kind is explained in the picture captions on pages 64–67. Each of the pictures was drawn by two older children, with each one choosing an animal and becoming one with it. The two 'animals' agreed to communicate by gestures. Are they going to quarrel? Let us first try to draw a quarrel between ourselves be-

62 c

62 d

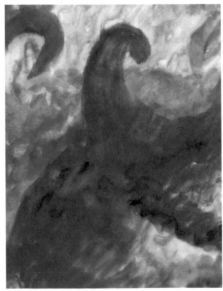

63 a–c *What does handwriting tell us?* Perhaps what we have come to understand from watching animals. The children may write the word 'giraffe' in yellow-brown with long legs or the word 'snake' crawlingly. The mouse handwriting should be tiny, grey, round and crooked; the word 'parrot' should shout merrily; the kangaroo handwriting should be jumpy but different to that of a flea's. The word 'elephant' should walk in grey dignity and rounded shapes.

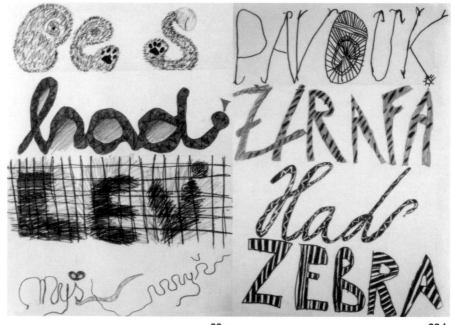

63 a   63 b

fore we put fur or feathers into the picture. We sketch the stiff gestures of a quarrel on paper. Perhaps this will lead to an interesting clinching of paws, wings or beaks. To be able to draw the fur or feathers more quickly, take a twig flattened with a hammer. It could be submerged in Indian ink. It might work just as quickly with a bundle of skewers or an old toothbrush. Try it yourselves. We recommend you start drawing the fur from the edge of the shape of the animal to make it flexible, and don't forget that even fur and feathers have their logical growth. You shouldn't scribble in all directions. Try to get

63 c

71

64 a b c

64 d

the expression of the animal. What does it tell you? Am I very lazy, angry or excited? Speaking of expressions, which dog do you think looks the happiest, the most furious and the most worried? I'll tell you a joke: 'Buy a basset. When you get home the dog will look as if it had more worries than you.'

When we tried to sign our name like a dog or create a dog's face, we always had a specific breed in mind. When we were lost for words we went back to the exceptional qualities captured by Karel Čapek in his book *I had a Dog and a Cat*. Judge for yourselves how Karel Čapek was able to watch and understand a dog. A St Bernard, for example: '... inhumanly serious and spectacularly noble, lazily moving in his too large and too shaggy skin ... softly and stately he trudges along, to again warm his solitary melancholy in the sun.' And a schnauzer or small terrier: '... with a nice beard, shaggy, hairy, bristly and the colour of pepper and salt, as agile as a boy and happy as a man, a big fighter and guardian ...with the most merry eyes in the world.'

Karel Čapek did not only compare dogs, but also tried to find the difference between 'catness' and 'dogness'. His characterisations of a cat and a dog

64 a–c *How do people dress up to look like animals?* Just think of the masks of shamans and magicians, totems or human beings turned into animals by a spell. You will also find creatures in fables who are half human and half animal. In our big masks, painted with the help of colour prints on an axis, we can see the Monkey King (a), Minotaurus (b) and the Bird King (c).

64 d *The totem* was made from a symmetrically drawn name, written vertically on a vertically folded piece of drawing paper. This is the personal guardian of the author. Can you read the name? (Šárka.)

65 a, b *The attraction of mysteries.* Does Yeti exist? Children and adults both like secrets and mysteries. Researchers found a tadpole in the water of a bromelia leaf, where a frog had left it, at the top of a tree in the tropics. They also found desert frogs able to last until the rains came. They also found crustaceans and insects in caves breathing hydrogen sulfide. Why would creatures not exist in the Himalayas? Yeti became popular because he is mysterious. A student created a sunbathing Yeti with his own cap and glasses. For the masks of the funny looking Yetis, the pupils of the seventh class only needed one hour, telling their friends how they manage to live in the cold of the Himalayas. They live well enough, if only people would leave them alone. Would you like to try another mystery — the Loch Ness monster — on the computer? Hunt for it and find it with the sonar?

65 a

are worth quoting: '... the cat is of the family of ironists who have fun with themselves, they play with people and things only for their internal and somewhat contemptuous pleasure. The dog is of the family of jokers: he is good-

65 b

73

66 a

hearted and vulgar like one who likes to tell jokes and would die of boredom without an audience ... The cat is satisfied with its own experience, the dog wants to have success ... the cat is mysterious like an animal, a dog is naive and simple like man ...' In our creative endeavours we imagined ourselves with our masks, signatures, and communications to be in the realm of animals. There is something we should never forget, however. Animals were not created for people. Perhaps the following quote from *The Whale – the Ruler of the Sea* will help us all to realise this: '... Dr Lilly in vain tried to teach the

66 b

66 a *Fin-winged sharpbeak*. That is the name the little author gave his fantasy fish that will surely be discovered by someone in the depths of the ocean. If you would like to gain inspiration for a similar drawing, look in the atlas of fish where you can find the *Ogcocephalus vespertilio*, the seahorse, perch, diodon, or the Australian tunny-fish. You can change them a little and your atlas of extraordinary fish can go to print.

66 b *Jigsaw puzzle*. Nature seldom creates something nonsensical that cannot survive. It gives animals the chance to metamorphose; to adjust to their environment. Some birds dive, while fish, on the other hand, can fly. This little artist is presenting nonsense on purpose, however. Only in fairytales do dragons with several heads exist, while myths contain combined animals. Can you find parts of various animals in this picture and draw their remaining parts? What would a little bird, dog or pig made from this puzzle look like?

67 a, b *Computer mice drawn with computer mice*. People sometimes live like mice. They eat cheese, have supplies in the larder and a cosy room with a telly and computer. From morning till night they look at the screen and imagine that the world is just a tiny village that they know intimately. But what happened? Just look at our pictures. The screen turned into a mirror: 'You are an ordinary mouse,' the screen says.

'Come out of your computer room. The sun is shining, the trees are blossoming; you must touch, feel and see the world for yourself.'

67 c, d *'Draw Pegasus,'* whispers the screen, 'so that you can see the world with eyes from above. Look at it as a fantasy. Pegasus is the means of transport for poets.' I took a few children for a walk around a house we knew well. We had some paper and each one wrote down what they saw, touched, felt and heard. When we read of the interesting discoveries it was almost like a poem: a dark, heavy door banged, behind it the blue sky. The white cloud is like a kite, tickled by a tree without leaves.

dolphins English, but dolphins speak exclusively "dolphinic". The new language has to be learnt and I see no reason why people could not manage "dolphinic".' What can we add? Birds, ants and fish in the fairytale about Goldilocks speak and say what they think about people.

What would storks and butterflies actually tell us? Nothing! But let us not be sad. It is up to us to understand, by long observation, how animals communicate, express happiness and show they are well. Let's try to save their environment and living conditions and thus save our own existence. Their lives with us, the 'civilised animals', are not easy. Not a single animal species, however, knows (or is interested in knowing) how difficult communication between people is, how difficult it is for nations, various human communities and even two partners who want to start a family, to come to an agreement. Do you know how young males in the animal kingdom attract the favour of the females? The crab waves one of his large claws, a certain type of spider plays on his web, the colours of a male fish shine brightly and the lizard starts to swing. We can read in scientific literature about the elegant

68

and sometimes funny songs and dances of mating birds. They try to attract attention with their movements, sound, colours, light and smell. Miss Night Butterfly lures her partners from miles away with her perfume – pheromone. What about drawing or painting the wooing and weddings of various birds, butterflies, fish and lizards?

Do you know which animal communicates with light – the so-called bio-luminescence? Fireflies blink at various time intervals to recognise a member of their family. In South and North America lives the skipjack. If he displays two green lights in front, it means that he is resting. If he blinks the back red light, it means, 'Attention, I am flying!' One summer night the children took some torches and transparent coloured cellophane and performed a circular colour ballet on a sloping meadow. The artistic 'light' performance was successful. For many artists light is also a means of expression. Try to quietly talk to the light. You can also do this with torches in a room.

Whatever animal species stimulates the children in their creative activities, the motivation for their art should also include something of the real knowl-

69 *A tamer or Mowgli?* You can choose and paint either. The two children who painted this large picture decided that they would rather be tamers. Mowgli, even though he understood the jungle, killed the big, dangerous cat, but they prefer to tame it. We can talk to children about how the 'family of cats' lives in the natural world; how they feel in circuses and zoos; how a predatory animal becomes a cannibal; why small cats cannot 'bawl' like a lion; and why their eyes are shining.

69

edge of the particular animal species. In the spirit of 'understand and protect', we refer to three international organisations and their principles: The International Union for the Protection of Nature (UICN), The World Wildlife Foundation (WWF), The UN Ecological Programme (UNEP).

The principles can be summarised:

1   Limit the intensity of the thoughtless exploitation of fauna and flora.

2   Do not take extreme measures that lead to the decrease of oxygen in the atmosphere and fertility of the oceans.

3   Maintain the diversity of animal and plant species.

70

70 *A winged horse.* This time it is not a computer drawing of Pegasus, as on page 75, but a painting by a small child. Note the contrast of light and warmth and the dramatically conceived space. We wanted to close the chapter with this picture. It represents the freedom of animals and people. In fairytales people reward animals and animals reward people. Humans understand the language of animals, and animals can speak the human tongue.

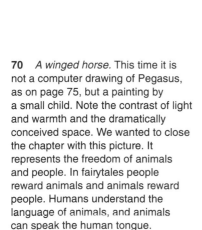

A

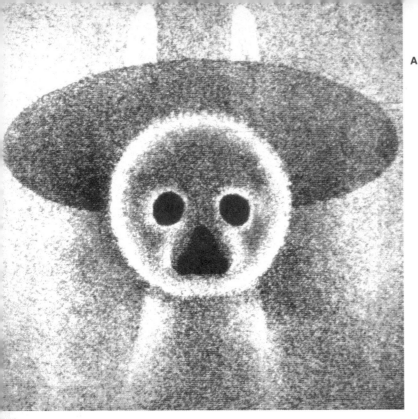

 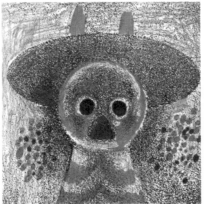

▼ B

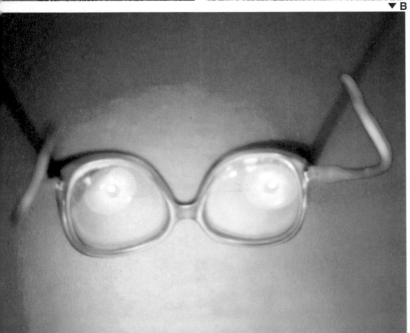

C

A **Petr Nikl** (born 1960), *A face,* 1995, tapestry, 250 x 245 cm. Look at it and try to remember where you saw this face. Perhaps a memory of teddy bear childhood? Or an extra-terrestrial from the moon? Maybe a portrait of the visionary rabbit from the wise book by Richard Adams, *Watership Down* (published in 1972). We made copies of the exhibition catalogue and children of the second class completed the rabbit. He is called April.

B *How a strange beetle frightened me.* All that was needed was a lamp and glasses. I called the children to come and have a look at what is watching me.

C *Cat's writing*, thought the children taking a walk about the Vyšehrad, who looked at the wall made up of various stones and bricks. They tried to interpret its message on the stone and made a rubbing of it.

D *Report on a swallow.* In the summer the wind blew a swallow down our chimney. It fell 15 metres through the pipes and started to rustle in the cold stove. Its wings black with soot, it started to paint our white kitchen ceiling before it found its way out through the window. Who else can boast that a small Phoenix flew out of their ashes and painted frescoes on their walls? We shall leave the frescoes where they are. (The rain washed the dirt off the swallow, but we still often wonder what it felt like in the chimney.)

E *What can this nosey swan confirm?* It walked with us as far as the river Vltava. I carried a bag with a small carp Joe to put him back in the river on Christmas Eve. The children thought that Joe would stick his head out from under the water and thank them, but it was the swan who thanked instead of him. It stretched its neck, and did not want to have its more beautiful photo taken from the side.

D

F   *A stone fish.* We saw it in one of the parks (Chotek Park). It let the children ride on its back. Perhaps the children really wanted a reward for returning the carp to the water. Why could there not be any mysteries in one of the oldest parks in Prague? The stone fish will certainly still be there when these children bring their grandchildren to look at it.

G   *Visitors.* I am sure you often go to the zoo, but which children are lucky enough to have the animals come to school? Take a good look at the animals and work out which species they are. Try to determine whether such a visit to your school would be good or bad. Write your opinion in two columns under 'good' and 'bad', clarifying each opinion. But verify each of your opinions. Call the zoo or read about llamas, and you will find out which animals could be kept at school and under what conditions.

E

G

F

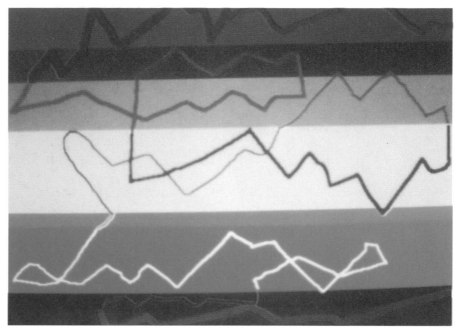

72

Other People and I

How come I am what I am? Mothers, fathers and children. What did we inherit from our forefathers? The mysteries of our brain. The art of seeing, hearing and feeling. The art of communication and getting to know oneself.

Some twelve-year-old children once told me that they are 'scared' of themselves. Sometimes, before they fall asleep, they become aware of themselves as 'I'. They asked whether I also had a self, an 'I'. I assured the children that every self has problems and pleasures. We are conscious of ourselves. Our freedom lies not only in the right to say and do what we want, but in being able to imagine ourselves in the place and experience of others.

We held hands in a circle and sent signals by squeezing each other's hands. The children made up new signals. We sent each other signals by making faces and using our hands. Later everyone added something and an interesting alternative was the sending of smiles or some kind of touch expressing pleasure and friendship. We also tried to simulate gestures of fear, surprise and sadness and act out the following situations: I walk in the dark and something frightens me, I call for help, I open a present, I am surprised and pleased, I want to score a goal or throw the ball into the basket, but I don't succeed.

Is it possible to draw or paint such a situation in a more interesting way than simply as an illustration of a scene? The children tried it by tracing their own shadows on an asphalt path in the park (pictures 71, 91 a–c). They

71 *Combination.* The sun was shining on the path in the park and the children could outline their shadows. The task was clear. They were supposed to draw, according to their shadows, how they pass a ball into the basket, how they do gymnastics, and what they are doing together. Making a 'sculptural group' of their shadows was certainly not easy, and together they had to try various alternatives to make the figures decipherable. In the picture you can see how three boys put a large drawing together with the help of their shadows. It was supposed to be a situation in which the well-known Michael Jordon of the Chicago Bulls runs for the basket.

72 *Handing over the relay.* Older children tried a situation on the computer in which a person knows something but may not be able to pass it on. It doesn't matter if somebody loses their way, it is just important to deliver the news. Two children took turns using the mouse. You will find other stages of this discussion on pages 100–101.

81

73 a

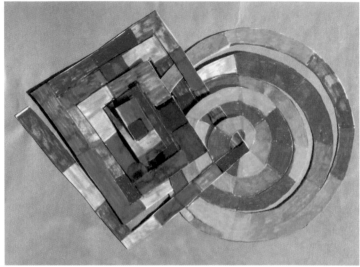

73 b

ascribed various meanings to their gestures and then phased them. It was possible to draw a linear graph on the computer which showed breathing in and out when all is calm, then showing it speeding up when playing sport or during a sudden change of the psyche such as an intense experience of fear or pleasure. How can one portray the beating of the heart? Let's hold the wrist of our friend with the left hand and draw with our right hand the beating of their pulse using the mouse and graphic program. We then exchanged the roles of patient and doctor. Which of the doctors is also an interesting artist?

73 a, b *Two people are fond of each other.* After an interesting discussion the children agreed that anyone who knows how to love gives something, but also remains whole. They receive what they get with pleasure. The children drew pictures of intertwined hands, shadowed profiles and wedding photographs. The older children were more abstract in their drawings. We would like to show you two examples from the many alternative computer graphics made by a ten-year-old girl (a), and a collage of two shapes which an older boy cut out in the form of a spiral then folded together (b).

74

74 *When Peter is born.* Peter is happy inside his mother. He feels as if he is in an Easter egg and is growing nicely. Before he is born he turns so that his head if facing down. At the age of three he begins nursery school, he lives in a nice house and will stay there even after he gets married. He will have two children. The teacher in school will have no complaints. (The picture was made and the description written by a ten-year-old girl after a discussion on parenthood.)

75 *Microbaby.* The origin of life can also be depicted between two foils. The children placed a drop of oil colour in a small frame made of blotting paper. When projected, the drop moved like a living cell many times enlarged.

76 a *Triplets* were drawn by a nine-year-old boy, who already had four siblings. He was the last one. He thought it might have been good if three of them had been born on the same day. They would come from the same form, from one egg, and nobody would be able to tell them apart. They could have a lot of fun.

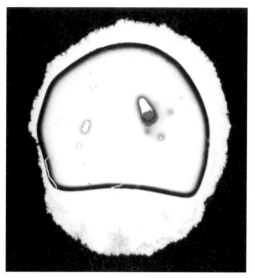

75   76 a

If the children have several computers at their disposal then there are other opportunities for transcription. A record of the body's rhythm can be made choosing the most effective lines and colours from the KID-PIX program. The picture of the artist could be made up of several different graphs: how I breathe; how my heart beats; how often do I blink? What does a cough look like? Between the various stages the children can look at other monitors and see how others record their breathing. Some record it as if they were struggling up a hill than going down into a valley. Others graphically blew up and

76 b

76 b *Twins.* Little Peter floats in a light blue colour. He will be named after his grandfather. Zdenka floats in pink and will be named after her mother. She will be born on the first of April, on All Fools' Day, and is looking forward to it. She looks forward to meeting her father and mother. They will live in a beautiful house with a garden and a dog.

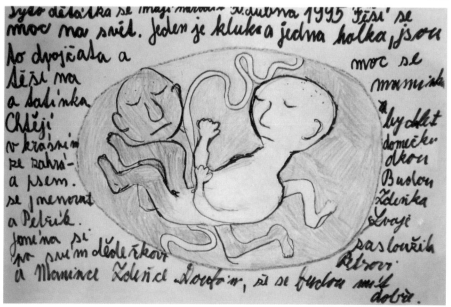

83

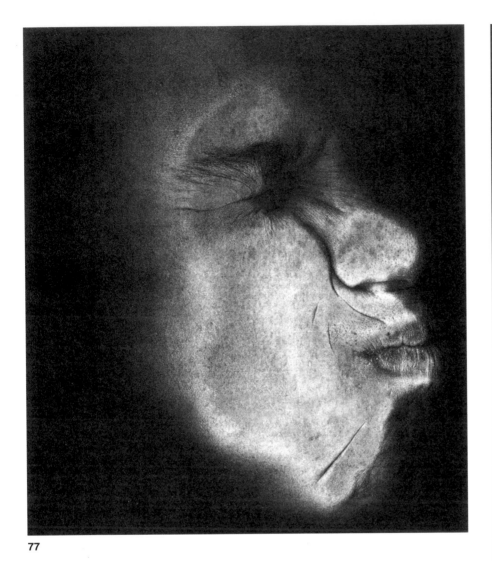

77

77 *My ancestor the anthropoid.* Put your face on the photocopier, purse your lips, close your eyes and you can have a lot of fun. Could we make less distorted profiles from the photocopy? Computer, try and work out how many ancestors our anthropoid would have!

deflated a balloon, while another record looked like a sheet of music. Some recorded the blinking of eyelids by alternating negatives and positives in squares, while others made their whole picture flutter. One child recorded his blinking with black circular areas for when, as he said, it was dark behind the eyelids. How many heartbeats did you count in one minute? If you were a mouse you would count 500 beats, but if you were an elephant it would be only 20–25 beats per minute. What information can be derived from these figures?

The greatest number of graphic symbols appear on the monitor when recording the beating of the heart. Whether the children see it as a string of beats or a wavy horizontal line running in a vertical direction, red is most often the colour used. The children consider breathing to be blue. It's interesting to compare how many breaths, blinks and heartbeats appear on the monitor in a given period, for example, one minute. If the children do not have a computer, why not draw their rhythms with crayons on paper? It will certainly be interesting for the children to compare the artistic recordings of the body

78 *A pretty girl can also turn into a witch.* How? When she is rude, hateful, evil, envious and wanting everything for herself. It seems requires no skill to be born, but it is an art to age wisely starting the minute we are born. The enlarged profiles began with the smallest and youngest. The boy then put all the profiles in one 'book' and this made an interesting sculpture.

78

rhythms of various people. A person breathes and blinks like a cat or black-bird but is a more complicated animal. A cat or blackbird never ask why and how something exists. They never write a scientific thesis or a poem, nor do they paint a picture. Humans with their 100,000 genes or units of inherited information, are comprised of three intertwined strands: sensibility, reason, and ability to differentiate between good and evil. There are many complications; and do we become wiser in the labyrinth of everyday life? This depends not on the person themself, but also on the wise people they meet in their life.

What were we like in the beginning? Children of the fifth class had several sessions on parenthood with a wise doctor. She told them about their birth, about the love of two people and the responsibility of bringing up a child. The children were naturally very interested in what they were like before they were born, so we tried to explain the birth of a child using the language of art. The children imagined a kind of Fairy Godmother as in the fairytale Sleeping Beauty. The Fairy Godmother would, however, be surprised to see that the

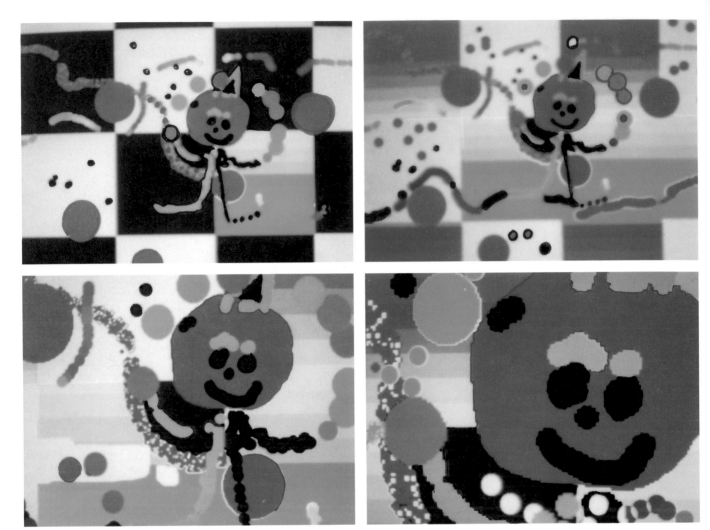

79 a b
   c d

children drew the subject 'What kind of baby will you be?' in a very enlightened way. They didn't draw the Sleeping Beauty's cradle, but a micro-cosmos of babies in their mothers. Have you seen the beautiful cradle in the picture by the photographer Lennart Nilson? The world press compared his photos of babies before birth to photos of the far side of the moon. In the 1970s, NASA sent the series of photographs about the birth of a child out into the universe along with other information about our solar system, with the help of Voyager I and II. Since there are such miracles as photos of babies within the micro-cosmos of their mothers, why not show them to the children? It has been proven that a child before birth has already developed senses; it perceives, judges and even has a memory. When the baby is seven weeks old it reacts to a touch, to fondling. In the twentieth week it becomes a listener, later calming down when it hears a lullaby or a soothing tune it remembers. The samples on pages 82, 83 and 86 show that it is possible to encourage the love of and respect for life.

These drawings of babies before birth are permanently exhibited in the corridor of the maternity clinic. The sensitive doctor took the children's draw-

79 a–d *Doctors can see the unborn baby* on a monitor. Why don't we try to re-create the stages of growth of a happy little creature on the computer? The artistic approach could be interesting.

79 a *You see, now it is playing chess* with its father and mother. It will be clever!

79 b *Or is its mother singing?* Can you see how happy it is?

79 c *It can even do somersaults* like a clown.

79 d *Perhaps it is trying to hum and purr* happily like a kitten.

80 a *How do our hemispheres talk to each other?* They are connected by many hundreds of millions of filaments. The children tried to draw the shape of the brain and complete it according to a photocopy. The left hemisphere contains perception, understanding and logic. The right is more of an artist: it experiences emotions, distinguishes metaphors, creates music and has a sense of humour. The boy shows the difference with the help of two colours; the wise in blue and emotions in red.

80 b *How does a girl perceive and experience a flower?* Two children represented this in a collage. The glued-on parts with the birds are memories of the one who gave the girl the flower. (You will find similar collages on pages 92 and 93.)

80 a

80 b

ings with her as they reminded her of the trust and pure openness of the children she had met.

Reason is one of the traits that makes humankind different: a rational and self-aware animal able to see the difference between good and evil, truth and lies. Hold your head in your hands; that is where reason resides. We made photocopies of the human brain and started to think artistically. What about? About a tree, for example. If neurologists say that the right half of the brain is more artistic, experiences and distinguishes emotions, writes poetry, has a sense of humour and appreciates music, wouldn't it be right to draw a picture of it as a tree full of colours and fairytale birds? Let's write down other metaphors of this tree on the right hand side of the paper. It could be a hand that waves to us, a mysterious town with a cursed people or a concert hall with an orchestra of birds, perhaps.

For the left hemisphere of the brain which takes care of perception and logic, we could draw a particular tree and describe it by species as we have learnt in Nature study.

When playing with the picture of the brain, the children worked independently. Some drew the personification of their senses around the photocopy: hearing with long ears, sight with large eyes, feeling with big hands, smelling with a big nose and taste with the tongue stuck out (picture 81). Other

81

82 a

children cut the photocopies up and created fantastic beings out of the pieces: a collage of the Wise Old Man, evil portrayed as a naughty devil while good took the shape of a fluffy kitten. Some children wrote lies around one side of the photocopy and important truths around the other. It was interesting that the children intentionally chose dangerous lies and contradicted these lies with the truth. All the subjects had something to do with ecology and humanitarianism. The older children then openly discussed the two opposites: lies and truth. On a more abstract level, it was possible to express in colour how, in the brain, 'evil' fights 'good', the 'kind I' sits alongside the 'egoistic I', and the 'frightened I' is beside the 'courageous I'. Clearly the children did not consider themselves uniform beings: the hero who is not afraid doesn't really exist. In overcoming fear, cowardliness and egoism, the real courage and heroism of humankind can often be found. The struggle of good and evil takes place in every person. We tried to animate the dialogue of the two opposites, good and evil, cowardliness and courage, on the computer. A more complicated alternative can be found on pages 100–101. Try for yourselves, perhaps in an abstract form using a pencil, the subject: 'How a wolf turned into a sheep'.

Every one of us is different and we differ not only in what we look like and in our temperament, 65 per cent of which is inherited. Our character is mainly formed by the environment into which we are born, however, and also by

81 *The brain of Bara of the 5th class.* The children had photocopies of the human brain in simplified black and white drawings. We talked about its mysteries such as the fact that memory is connected with the five senses, or that a child knows about 6,000 words by the age of six. An average person knows 14,000. Information in the long-term memory is stored in nerve cells in the outer part of the brain. We looked at them enlarged a thousand times: a marvellous and miraculous store! The children drew their miracle, with everyone drawing what they considered most important. Bara, as you can see, personified her five senses as sprites. Do you recognise hearing, smell, sight, taste and touch?

82 a–c *This is the 5th class.* One of our friends outlined our heads on a piece of paper. We then drew by

82 b

82 c

memory, the help of two mirrors and the sense of touch. Around our portraits we wrote what can be read from our faces: what we want to be, what we like to do and what we inherited from our parents and grandparents.

82 a *I am Martin Pertl* and I would like to be a fireman. I inherited my kind of hair from my father. I would like to know how to play the drums.

82 b *I am Eliška Bucvanová*. I am eleven years old. My hobbies are dogs and music. I have a dog, Deni, and a budgie.

82 c *My name is Ondřej Melena.* I am in the 5th class. Like my mother I am dyslexic. I inherited blue eyes from my grandfather. I like to ride bikes and I am strong. I am good at sports like my mother.

learning. Let us, for example, look at the children in a classroom who are the same age, and determine the colour of their eyes and hair, their height and build. It can be great fun to classify the children according to their traits, and we are sure to find such opposites as a small blue-eyed girl with fair hair and a curly haired boy with black eyes who is much taller. Can we draw their portraits and show how they differ?

What did we inherit from our ancestors? How are we similar to them? We tried to find out by looking at portraits of ourselves. The children brought some photographs of their relatives and spread them across a big table: great-grandfathers, great-grandmothers, grandfathers and grandmothers, fathers and mothers. Some even brought two of each person; one from when they were children and one from when they were older. First we looked at the photos of the relatives as babies or children, trying to find out what had been handed down in their gene code. Dark eyes and hair? A round face? The total expression of the face? We then looked at the photos of the relatives as adults. Will we look like that when we grow up? Let's draw grandmother or grandfather before we start our own portrait.

When looking at the photographs it was not only a question of the external image; it was also interesting to find out what the children remembered, what their relative did and whether people liked them. We put the grandmoth-

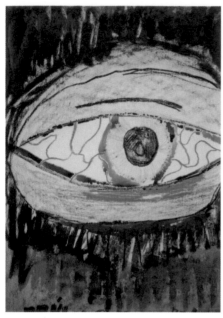

83 a

83 b

83 a, b *The eye – a window to the heart.* Try to place a piece of paper over your face so that only one eye can be seen. Can people tell your expression by your eyes? What does the expression of the eyes look like when laughing, crying, afraid, hating, being cruel or, on the other hand, being gentle and kind? We enlarged one eye and showed what kind of person this is with the help of wax crayons over the computer drawing. I am sure you can recognise (a) a 'sad eye' and (b) a 'cruel eye'. The latter does not like fairytales, but prefers horror movies. It seems that cruelty has the upper hand in such a person. Take care when you hear his funny 'Hello'. We know that doctors can detect not only the age but also diseases from the eyes. Try to 'speak' using only your eyes. Say: I've got it! Don't tease me! I knew it! Halloooo!

ers who told the children fairytales into a group, while other groups comprised those who liked to sing or played a music instrument. In another group were grandmothers who were marvellous cooks and there were also sporting relatives who were good skiers, football players or swimmers. One rare grandmother climbed rocks and taught her grandson to climb. Another rather large group consisted of drivers, and also gardeners. The sons of three fishermen

84

84 *Mother's perfume?* Do you recognise it? The perfume reaches your nose like a beautiful rainbow. Try to hide a perfume somewhere in the classroom. Which child can smell it first? We need not try only the perfume of flowers. Let's try to hide burnt potatoes with garlic. You can let this bad smelling spirit out in the classroom and it may create exciting paintings. Do you have any other ideas? I remember one boy drew the theme of The Wise Old Man fairytale: 'I can smell something human. Who have you got here, Mother?'

85 a *Alarm clock, friend or foe?* The last sound you hear before falling asleep might be the ticking of a clock. How can something so quiet that we didn't notice all day now be heard so clearly?

85 a

85 b

85 b *In the morning the alarm rings* till our ears hurt. Wouldn't it be better if some pleasant music woke us? We have got a musical alarm clock at home, left by our grandmother. It plays a tinkling melody and if it doesn't put you to sleep, it certainly makes waking up more pleasant.

86 *A terrible noise* can easily be painted or drawn, but it isn't so pleasant to listen to. Do you know that people become aggressive when there is too much noise? Agitated children are less able to concentrate. If the noise is constant, hearing becomes less sharp.

The Greek philosopher Plato certainly did not have brawling and disharmony in mind when he said, 'Musical education is a far more effective educational tool than any other, because rhythm and harmony find a way to the secret places of the soul.'

told the others about their catches, children of musicians tried to put together an orchestra consisting of their relatives. Every family has its thrilling story which the children have heard many times or even experienced. They could write or draw it.

Something similar can be done at home and will be greatly enjoyed by your own children or grandchildren. The album of photographs suddenly comes alive with the details of our own faces, skills and actions. It depends on us how we portray a happy grandmother who, in the photo, is looking at her grandson dressed as a masked man. Perhaps a child will be inspired by a photo of his uncle standing in front of an easel. Why not draw these interesting relatives and put the drawing alongside the photos in the album? When the children drew their own portraits, their comments showed that they had

86

87 a

87 b

been thinking about all that they inherited from past generations. When they described what they like to do or what they want to be, we can see that their interests have their roots in the family. You can find three of these portraits on pages 88 and 89.

Everybody is interested in who they are. We can't discover this by looking at our reflection in the mirror or at the lines in the palm of our hand. The various schools of psychology find different explanations. People wonder whether they are choleric or melancholic, sanguine or phlegmatic; I wonder if they may know that Hippocrates studied his temperament in the 4th century B.C. The professor of genetics and psychiatry from Washington University in St Louis, C. R. Cloninger, presented an interesting model of the psychology of humankind in 1993. Let's try to use his theory of 'measuring' perception, thoughts and communication on a graph. Older pupils or students will consider this an interesting way to get to know themselves or to at least come to understand the actions and expressions of people they know.

Let's draw seven cups (they are actually columns of the same size used to measure contents between 0% and 100%). The first four cups measure

87 a–d *Flowers and girls*. The collage on the double page was made by children who put pictures from several calendars together. From one they got portraits of ladies painted by painters, from the second they took pictures of girls in advertisements, while the third offered pictures of still-lifes with flowers. The children tried to create a new picture. The base was the face of a woman, while the background was comprised of flowers. We put the completed collages next to each other. How did they differ? The children decided that this was actually a description of the relationship between the girls and flowers, and also of those who gave them the flowers. What are these girls thinking? The children suggested:

87 c

87 d

87 a '*I think of you and I feel sad.*'

87 b '*Why did not you stay with me* instead of leaving the flowers in your place?'

87 c '*Nobody can buy me* with flowers.'

87 d '*That woman is blind* when it comes to flowers. Flowers wither from pride as in that fairytale about the Proud Princess.'

our temperament, which we mostly inherit from our ancestors. We shall try to fill the cups with different amounts, colouring them with crayons according to what we know of ourselves and our responses:

1   The first cup concerns our desire to search for that which is new. Let's see how inquisitive we are and how much we want to explore our environment.

2   The second cup measures our inclination to avoid pain. Are we willing to take risks or are we afraid of the future, other people and our own inertia?

3   The third cup should be filled according to how much we crave rewards: how much we want to be recognised and how much we depend on the approval of others.

4   The fourth cup measures our perseverance. How do we challenge our laziness or inertia?

The remaining three cups deal with our character: the set of morals with which we consider ourselves to be part, not only of humankind, but also of Nature and the universe. We fill these three cups according to how we are influenced by our environment and education:

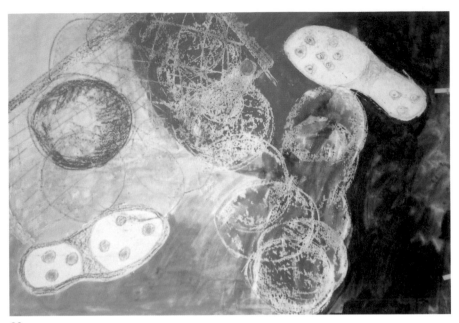

88 a

88 a, b *Sports games.* That is also about communication, where much depends on the ability to reach an agreement quickly. An instant reaction must be decisive. It means tension, excitement and enjoyment for the players and those who watch them. As in life, however, it is sometimes more important to know how to lose. If the players are able to communicate, does the same apply to the fans? The children made a whole series of drawings on the occasion of 'The Day of the Ball' organised by the school.

88 a *Pass me the ball and I'll score a goal.* Wax crayon drawing later painted over with thin colours.

5   The first of the three cups measures the ability to examine oneself – how responsible we are for our actions, how strong our will is and whether we are able to trust ourselves.

6   The next cup should be coloured to measure our willingness to co-

88 b

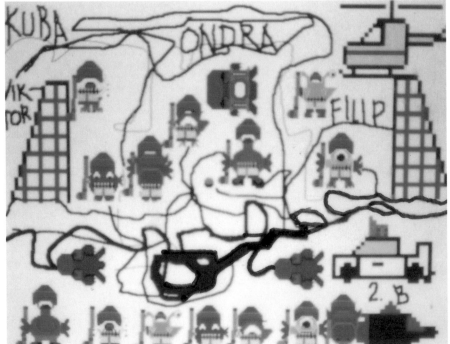

88 b *Ice-hockey.* Four boys from the second class sat in front of the computer. Each designed his on- and off-field outfits from the graphic program. They then went out on the ice and started to skate. According to the picture it seems that each is a strong individual who only plays by himself. They even signed their names in Czech (Viktor, Ondra, Kuba and Filip).

89 *Statues of two knights*. This is more of a reminder of the fame of knights on the tilting grounds of old, who fought in tournaments for the favour of one of the ladies. Lances were tossed and flags flew. The artists had to fight for these two angry knights. Which of them would be faster and blow his opponent away in one breath? The winner received a paper rose from his lady.

89

operate. Let's look at how much we respect the rights of other people, whether we quarrel for unimportant reasons, hurt, slander, seek revenge, experience envy, or look out only for our own advantage.

7   The last cup concerns reaching out or wisdom. It measures the abil-

90

90 *Space for life*. Does this look like a circus clown? It could be. We aimed to push our figure on a stick into the neck of a bottle, making sure that there was plenty of space left. Was it difficult for those who pushed their figures into the bottle last? Never mind. The order can be turned around with the first becoming the last.
A similar game can be played on the computer. Each can give advice to the others. Artists often call such an arrangement composing, harmonising or the balancing of opposites.

91 a

91 b

91 a–c *Icarus or swimmers?*
It's clear from all three pictures that the children composed and then outlined their figures and hand gestures. The shadow on the asphalt was elongated and distorted. In the classroom on paper, however, the children outlined their figures clearly. While the younger boys let their shadow fly or swim (a, c), the older children tried to compose their silhouettes in connection. From the long strip of paper you can see the part where two figures are kissing (b). If you had all day to play together with your shadows, you might even create a sun clock.

ity to experience and recognise one's own unity with Nature. This includes people who are naturally diligent, responsible and independent, not striving for power, money or fame. They usually have a great life, caring deeply for others and respecting every living thing.

Did you fill your seven cups with different amounts? Instead of the cups

91 c

92 *View of a crowd of people.* In the Czech film *When the Tomcat Comes*, the cat has magic glasses and can see what people are like at any given moment. Those in love and the good ones are red, the jealous ones are yellow, while boring and unpleasant ones are grey. Two girls tried a similar subject in a painting. They first painted coloured faces on a large piece of paper, completing them when the colour dried.

92

you could draw a landscape with seven hills of different heights. Which will be the highest? The truth lies not only in how you see yourself, but also how others who you know see you. It is said that what you wear or say does not make a person of you. What we really are can be seen from our actions.

The 'game with the cups' and Cloninger's theory of the seven-dimensional

93

93 *Double BAF.* The masks were made very quickly from plasticine, a pot and a lid. They have a purpose. A mask enables a person to communicate more directly and with a greater sense of humour. These two children, for example, are going to tell their grandmother what they would like for lunch, or they may want to amuse their grandfather. They can offer their special recipes from the magic kitchen as a 'pot and lid'. They can communicate with each other, turn to the spectator with a question or do a monologue. It's interesting that sometimes you can learn more from a child if they put on a mask and tell you what worries them while pretending to be somebody else.

94 a

94 b

94 a, b *A waterfall of letters and words.* The collage on a long strip of paper was made by the whole class. The children could use letters on stickers which we were given by an advertising agency. The letters could be taken off the stickers and placed on the paper. At first the children stuck the letters to the paper in a random way. There were more and more and they made up short words which, in this chaotic waterfall, were like safe islands of secret messages. For example, 'Love? Dust. Blanka. He does not guess, but I do.'

(a) detail, (b) total

personality model is too exacting for children. What else did the children learn in the pictures shown in Chapter 4? They artistically reflected on various con-nections – people's relationship with themselves and with Nature. They got to know themselves.

Our thoughts show that humankind is composed of biological, historical,

95

95 *Aeroplane in danger.* On the back side of a collage made of cut out letters and a drawing, the little author wrote, 'Damaged instruments. The pilot is flying over mountains. He tries to signal that he is in danger, but the signals are interrupted. The passengers are in a panic. The space around the plane shudders and shakes.' People in danger should remain cool and communicate clearly and accurately. Fear and panic always makes the situation worse, and it often shows up the real character of the person. Have you seen the film about the sinking of the Titanic?

96 a–c *Stages of discussions; the solution of problems.*

96 a *On the computer screen we can see a discussion* between four people. They want to solve a problem.

96 b *It seems that they are not yet quarrelling*, but are using clear arguments with their colours.

96 c *We have to take a close look at some important problems.* The artistic solution could continue through many more phases. Perhaps it is best when the four children solve a creative problem between themselves.

97 a–c *Consensus* means being of the same opinion, in agreement, a common attitude, cooperation. Disagreements start when three little children fight over a toy. The aggressive one wins and the two losers stick together. Disagreements will continue. How can we reach an agreement? Should we agree on rules? Let's think about the three stages of agreement created by the computer and discuss them.

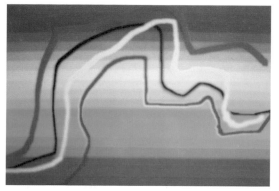

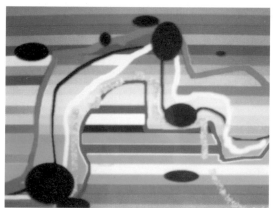

96 a b c

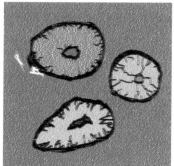

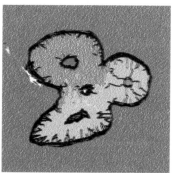

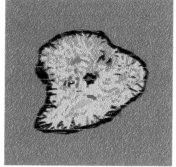

97 a b c

creative and ethical creatures. We live 'now' and we know that the daily situations, if we are open to their intensive, sensitive perception and handling, are much more concrete and individual. Real life cannot be programmed nor painted. There might come a significant moment, when our son or grandson must make an independent decision. What will be his decision which in a second adds up everything we were able to hand over to him in the generation cycle as his relation to values, which are indispensible for the quality of human existence? However, we are also pleased to learn the truth that the only good pupil is one who does not only copy his teacher.

Even if a son will not act in a specific situation as did his father or grand-

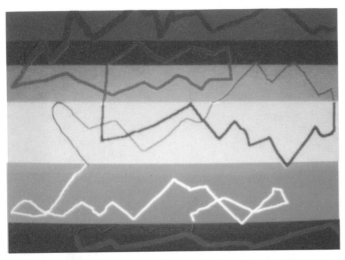

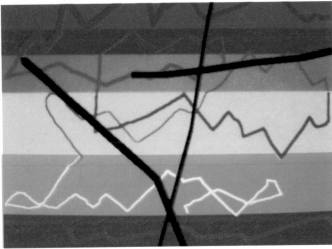

98 a b

98 a–f *A quarrel.* Computer graphics in six stages from the KID-PIX program.

98 a *A calm discussion.* Two children worked with the computer, taking turns with the mouse and holding a calm discussion in the coloured areas. The discussion was represented by a line and they moved along the line as in a relay.

98 b *Joining the discussion.* The third child played the role of the one who wants to quarrel. He crossed out the picture and thus disturbed the calm discussion.

98 c *A quarrel started.* The third child continued the sharp monologue with a wild black line. The other two children are only able to nervously run about between the thick lines. How can they stop the brute?

father, we know that human memory always goes back to the experiences of childhood without our realising it. The memory of a childhood that was kind, rich in experiences, activities, games is very intensive, colourful and sometimes is able to 'protect us' when we are grown up. (Before falling asleep I can still feel the safety of the garden, which I remember in detail. I am able to describe a scarf which my grandmother used as a magic prop when telling me a fairytale. I can recall the rare moments when my father allowed me to pick the first ripe peach from the tree, which, as a child, I had helped him to plant.)

All the time we put something in the memory of children. Let us guard that moment and try to understand that it is with the children that we experience some kind of adventure, which, after many years, can be again of interest to them when they became natural scientists, engineers, musicians, painters... and parents. The last, the seventh cup of 'wisdom' mentioned on pages 95 and 96 can be filled already during childhood. Humankind is not born wise, but becomes so. It is perhaps only Nature that knows our problem: however well informed we might be, we can never be quite sure of our wisdom.

98 c d
e f

98 d *We will freeze the quarrel!*
Enough! Nobody move! The children
make use of the computer program to
create a negative.

98 e *What about cutting the quarrel
into smaller pieces?* Will the picture
become calmer? On the contrary, the
muddle becomes even worse!

98 f *A quarrel doesn't lead
anywhere.* Any further cutting up of
the picture created an even greater
muddle. What now? The computer
can delete the whole picture. But what
about a real quarrel between people?
What do you suggest?

For further reading see: Cloninger, C. R., Sorakic, D. M, Przybeck, T. R.,
'A Psychological Model of Temperament and Character', *Arch. Gen. Psychiatry*, 50, 1993, pp. 975–990.

101

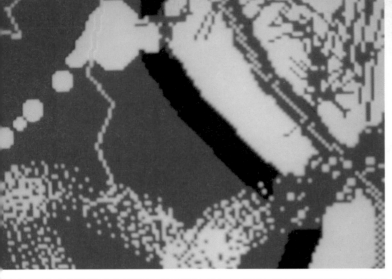

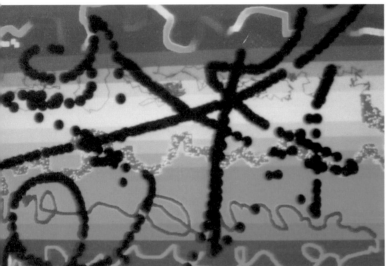

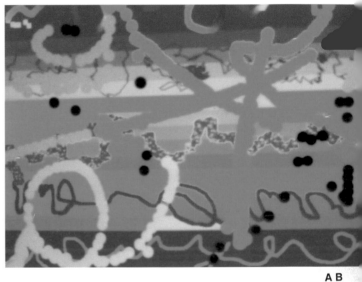

A B
C D

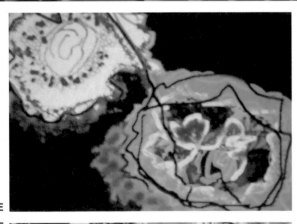

E

F

Students and future teachers tried to solve some problems on the computer with the KID-PIX program, even though they had had no previous experience. They worked in couples. They lent each other the mouse. Each student used half of the screen and chose their colours, lines and shapes for a certain mood and character.

A *Me and you*, a discussion on the boundary line (one phase).

B *Agreement* on the construction of the picture of a pyramid looking like an hour-glass.

C *The other one wanted to quarrel.*

D *How we avoided the quarrel.*

E *We differ* like the pictures of the agates, but we can come to an agreement.

F *Another alternative.*

G *'Keep quiet! Don't talk! Silence! I'm sleeping.'* Could you draw or paint a picture of 'sleep'? What do we actually see or hear when we are submerged in ourselves with eyes behind eyes? (Photographed at the request of the children, who were making drawings on the asphalt and suddenly became quiet.)

G

H

H Olbram Zoubek (born 1926). At the exhibition in Prague's Vojan Park, heroes from Greek mythology are taking a walk. They are not made of marble, but of cement. They quietly communicate with royal gestures, telling us about themselves and asking us what we know about them. The children went out to talk to them.

I *Communication.* 350 portraits, which the children exhibited in Neruda Street in Prague, surrounded the spectator. They were so close that you had to communicate with them whether you wanted to or not. 'Are you one of us? What are you actually like? What do you like to do best? What are you good at?'

I

5

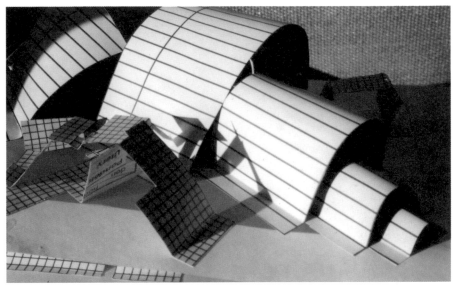

100

What will Remain of Us?

Pyramids, castles and telecommunication towers. Order or chaos? Holding a dialogue. An avalanche of information is not communication. The thumb of an astronaut. Why it is important to care, be informed, and able to help.

Over the course of time there have been many remarkable examples of human innovation: buildings made of stone and brick, ideas and innumerable moments of contact and communication. Let's try to document the wonders people have built by putting one stone on top of another.

When looking at scientific publications about the 'wonders of the world' – monumental constructions of ancient civilisations – we begin to wonder why they were built. Why did people work so hard? They built unbelievable monumental structures, next to which we are completely insignificant. They certainly did not build them because of the surplus of building materials such as stone; this was often dozens of miles away from the building site. It certainly was not easy to transport just one single ashlar, weighing about 138 tons, to a hilltop in Peru. Perhaps the most conclusive reason for these constructions was the fear that all humanity might disappear. Was faith or religion with its myths and rituals so compelling in its explanation of the order of the world, otherwise so difficult to understand, that humankind used it as a reason for their monumental constructions? The Tower of Babylon must have served as an observatory, while the Mexican monuments were calendars. They reflected the human desire to be assured of the order of Nature and the time granted by the universe. If the constructions in Peru made of hundred ton ashlars were palaces, cathedrals or graves, and the Egyptian pyramids were

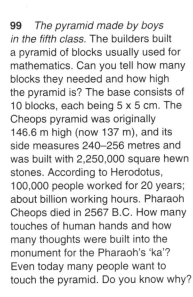

99 *The pyramid made by boys in the fifth class.* The builders built a pyramid of blocks usually used for mathematics. Can you tell how many blocks they needed and how high the pyramid is? The base consists of 10 blocks, each being 5 x 5 cm. The Cheops pyramid was originally 146.6 m high (now 137 m), and its side measures 240–256 metres and was built with 2,250,000 square hewn stones. According to Herodotus, 100,000 people worked for 20 years; about billion working hours. Pharaoh Cheops died in 2567 B.C. How many touches of human hands and how many thoughts were built into the monument for the Pharaoh's 'ka'? Even today many people want to touch the pyramid. Do you know why?

100 *Spacial construction.* Today's architects can dream and think about any kind of shape. They can turn the construction around on the computer. Would one like a 'dancing house'? He can create it. You can find it in Prague, on the Vltava embankment. Would another like a 'singing' opera house? He creates something that elegantly opens its mouth, resounding like a set of shells, spreading its wings like a bird. Here we have the Sydney Opera House, thanks to the magic of pre-stressed concrete. In their spacial constructions on simple white pads, the children tried to dream about the many possibilities of modern architecture. The picture shows a design for movable theatre stages.

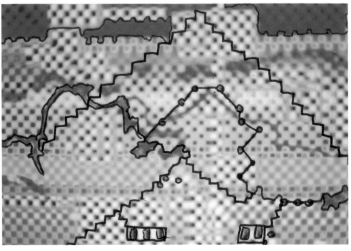

101 a

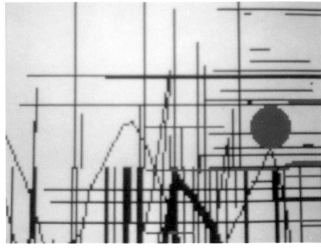

101 b

crypts, did humankind hope to overcome their fears through the monumentalisation of their constructions? Did they represent hope of eternal life? Three pyramids in Giza belonging to a father, son and grandson are monumental staircases leading to the universe. I wonder whether all three of the Pharaoh dynasty would've agreed that they were 'children of the stars' just as we are. I also wonder whether they would feel humble in the face of the universe or take pride in their place in the human race.

The children built a large pyramid of blocks, shown in the pictures 99 and 102, and we asked them why. In their answers we find their thoughts on human effort and behaviour: 'We built the pyramids because they were and still

102

101 a *Dreams about pyramids* can also be drawn on the computer. The children believed that the Pharaoh would be greatly surprised. Their first considerations revolved around the raster of the stones. The pyramid is drawn into the net, and the children considered certain layers of the construction in sections of time. They also thought about the internal arrangement of the passages: the irregular red passage is allegedly to show the Pharaoh how the burglars and researchers got into the pyramid.

101 b *Further thoughts concerning the pyramids* are actually more of a reflection on the relation of human beings to the sun. Human constructions such as towers and skyscrapers only rise above the sun when it is close to the horizon. You should know about this illusion of power, dear Pharaoh.

102 *A red pyramid.* This was built by girls. Can you see how it differs from the yellow pyramid made by the boys? How many blocks was it made with and how high is it? Many interesting mathematical problems were made up by the children on the basis of the two pyramids and their comparison. They thus connected the square and the cube with the experience of joint creation, communication and also with the interesting reading they did about the mysteries of ancient Egyptian art.

103 a   **103 b**

103 a   *How to talk with a castle and about a castle?* The stones in the computer drawing are put together as if they were letters in a coded message. What about constructing a castle on a prepared raster where the alternating of various coloured fields provides a kind of information?

103 b   *We can also build a castle with letters* forming the word CASTLE. The computer graphic program offers you the letters.

103 c   *Every castle has its happy and unhappy history.* Its history is black and white. We tried to create a black and white picture using the computer. The children had already drawn these two pictures and made collages on this subject.

are mysterious. They hide a secret. We wanted to know if we could do it. A pity we did not have more blocks. It let us talk with the Pharaoh. We're glad that the pyramids survived him.' The children then selected the best organiser, adviser and mathematician who created interesting problems and numerical puzzles based on the pyramid. He thus convinced the others that mathematics and geometry are actually quite marvellous. It's impossible to calculate the number of words and touches of hands needed for the construction of a pyramid. A persistent and cooperative sample of humanity was happy to create, to solve mysteries and to discover possible mathematical solutions in the order of construction: the children were persistent and co-

104 a

104 a *The image of a castle in a fairytale.* This is the castle which changes according to the fairytale Sleeping Beauty. The children tried several phases on the computer. At first the castle is white and decorated with garlands as the kingdom is happy about the birth of a little princess. Right from the beginning, however, a threat is present in the form of black Fate, leaving you to guess what the future of the unhappy castle will be. The green alternative tells us how, for a brief time, green hope won. The princess is 16 and nothing has happened yet.

operative. The children were proud of their pyramid when it was completed.

In the next stage of our research into cooperation in the building of large structures, we shall look at castles. Children like to draw and paint them. Sometimes they copy pictures, but more often they make drawings according to how they imagine a castle from a fairytale would look. We also tried to build simple castles on the computer screen; you can see them on pages 107 and 108. The advantage of computer drawings is the chance to make quick changes. The phasing of the drawing of a castle is based on the assumption that it would rest on a rock. The following phases can then show how the castle was damaged over the course of time. Other phases deal with

104 b

104 b *The castle suddenly turns black.* Fate has arrived and the princess has pricked her finger. This is not the end of the fairytale, however, and white memories remain among the black thorns. Can you imagine others in this series of castle pictures? Its liberation, for example, awakening from the hundred years' sleep and, finally, the happy wedding. (This was drawn by the children on large sheets of paper.)

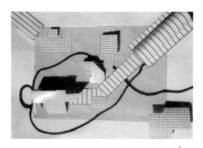

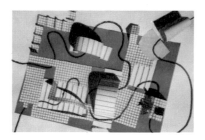

105 a, b *Theatres, sports centres, indoor swimming pools, schoolyards.* The children had these in mind when they made their designs out of paper pads. They used various lines and rasters which could correspond to the growth of a building as well as to the surface finish of tiles. They did not place a single building by itself, however, but considered where to place it within the environment of a lawn, sand pit or body of water. The small model represents a balanced, composed building. Wise buildings are beautiful because the form fulfils its purpose.

105 a *View of the theatre* from another side. This is the same work as in picture 100.

changes caused by a spell and its lifting, according to a certain fairytale. Several children can use one computer, taking turns with the mouse and making decisions as architects, magicians, conquerors or liberators. Why did people build castles? The answer seems to be the same as for the pyramids: people were afraid for their lives, but this time the threat came from other people. Do you know the saying, 'A person's house is their castle'? Every lord of a castle was proud of its impregnability and ostentation, and today children are delighted when they build a castle, even if it is only made of sand. Native Americans burnt their teepees when they thought they were going to die, but what about the lords of castles?

105 b

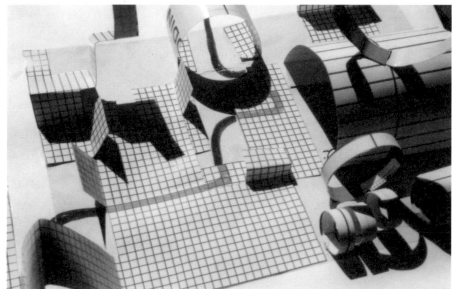

105 b *A sports centre* with a playing field and a small pool. Other solutions present other possibilities.

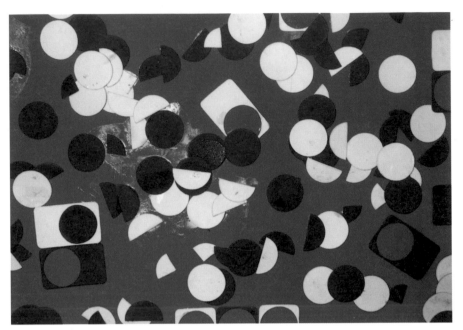

106 a

106 b

Other monumental structures such as temples and cathedrals were built in the Gothic style. Their common features are high vaults, cupolas and towers, all of which point towards the universe (just like the pyramids mentioned above). A person – even if an atheist – standing under the stately vault has a peculiar feeling of insignificance while still belonging to the universe. In no time people are often overcome with wonder and

106 a *Chaos*, which the children tried to create with geometric shapes in a particular area, is not only a random collection of wheels and rectangles on paper. Even here the children still had to compose their picture. Note that the blue, white and red colours appear in proportional rhythm within the format. Choose a place where you feel happy, even in this muddle, or another where you may feel sad or frightened.

The small picture humorously describes a kind of 'guardian of order' who does everything possible to be symmetrical. But he is not! It is enjoyable to look for deviations from the strictly proportional.

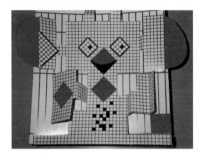

106 b *How chaos was put in order.* It's not a strict order and this is what makes the picture appealing. If the shapes were people, the people would have enough room to move freely. Somewhere two or four people sit comfortably around a table, couples are taking a walk and others are leading their small child. Where are you now in the picture? (The children worked under the supervision of a student teacher and this was her first school.)

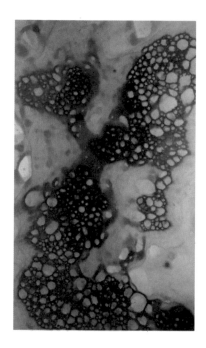

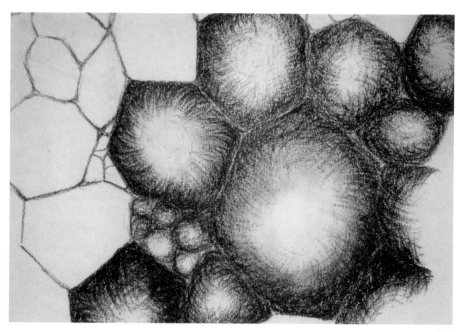

107 *Bubbles.* The inspiration for creative activity was an ordinary soap bubble. The students tried to make it visible. They put some coloured Indian ink into soap water, foamed it up with a quill and placed a tuft of bubbles on paper. You can see the result in the picture above left. What does it have to say and what does it remind you of? The texture of cells? A community of people? Perhaps even space/time foam (from which our bubble separated from the universe) which we talked about in Chapter 1? A structure has its order in the growth of shapes leaning on each other. Let's try to draw and understand the beauty and logic of the growth of honeycomb, crystals and other images of enlarged tissues.

108 *A knot and its mysterious bonds* can look like a complex problem which has to be solved with patience, by agreement and not with a sudden cut. Not every knot is a Gordian knot (that cannot be untied). It's important to think about how it was knotted and only then can it be untied. It's a good idea to draw a knot according to an interestingly knotted model, and to try to understand its construction in this way. Can you find the mistakes in the student's drawing? Where did the second 'output' rope come from?

pride that humankind was also able to build something so remarkable.

We must then mention the great structures of modern times. The children thought about them as they made their paper constructions using lined paper from their copybooks. You can look at these constructions in the pictures 100 and 105 a, b. When the geometrical lines were folded into curved planes, the children could imagine that the innovations of steel and concrete were

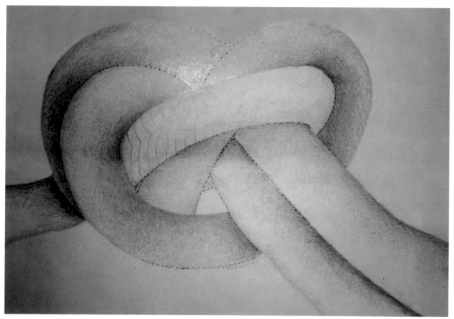

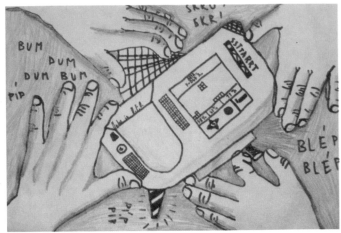

developments that delighted architects, builders and designers. Roads, bridges, dams, telecommunication towers, skyscrapers, prefab housing estates and cultural or sports centres are proof of the obsession with new technology. Do you know the secret of concrete? If you add water to cement, it reacts with the surface of the cement grains. A sort of jelly-like substance is created and after a few hours the cement grains start to grow and turn into crystals. These then join with the grains of sand and gravel. They bind so firmly that when they harden the concrete cannot be crushed.

Is concrete responsible for the wonders of modern times? Are the concrete monuments with protruding wires going to appeal to architects and archaeologists in another thousand years in the same way as the stone monuments of ancient civilisations? Perhaps we have to begin thinking about how we are

110

109 a *Communication when playing.* Drawing an agreement on the cooperative repair of a helicopter was easier for the children than actually repairing it. When building with building blocks they quarrel more often. It's always interesting to imagine how many human touches and communications the construction of a new object requires. In drawings a toy often serves as the model for the unfolding of a real life situation which the child may encounter.

109 b *We phone the extra-terrestrial.* The drawing tells us how the boys found a strange device with buttons, keys and screens. It proved to be a videophone made in a UFO. On one screen we can read in our own language what the ET is saying in sounds. On the second screen we can see what the ET looks like and is talking about. The children had to think of questions and answers for this unusual conversation. How would you introduce your planet and your home to an extra-terrestrial?

110 *My excavator.* The little three-year-old boy was so proud of this present that he showed it to everyone. Perhaps he even talked to it and slept with it and he certainly drew it with great skill. He enlarged what he most loved about the excavator — the huge shovel. Children and adults often talk to things but the methods differ. Have you heard a driver talk to their car or to their computers? They may speak both kindly and aggressively.

111 a–h *How we came to an agreement.* It should be a pleasure to come to an agreement with another person; to jointly solve a problem. Two older children used the KID-PIX program to describe a possible agreement in more than eight phases. You can see this on pages 113–115.

111 a *Each one of us is different.* Using the mouse, two boys divided the screen into two parts with a black boundary line. They used their imagination to complete their half of a picture, using their favourite colours and graphics from the program. They visited each other across the boundary line and thus created a joint point, a frontier pass. They soon decided that the whole picture was interesting and could stay that way, but why not see whether the two neighbours could agree on a joint solution to the whole area.

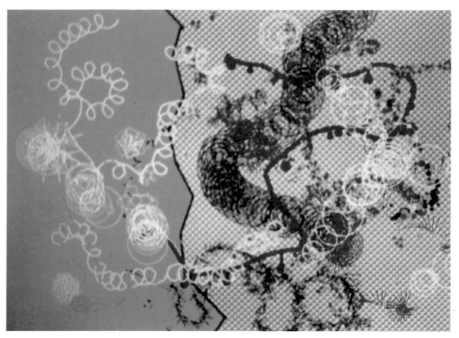

111 a

going to get rid of the concrete. The children suggested it be ground down and recycled so that something else could be built from it. They became unsure, however, when they looked at a picture of the Sydney Opera House, made of pre-stressed concrete, or at the CN Tower in Toronto, Canada. The latter is 553 metres high and rises daily by another six metres thanks to the climbing shuttering, which was raised by a hydraulic jack as the concrete hardened. We insisted that the children look from the inside and the outside

111 b

111 b *We have a common frontier pass;* a kind of junction where we meet. Let's take a closer look and enlarge it.

111 c

111 c *Let's take another look at the problem.* Further enlargement brought confusion. The linear structures cross each other but do not communicate. It even seems as if they are treading on each other.

at the jewel of concrete architecture – the chapel of Notre-Dame-du-Haut in Ronchamp by Le Corbusier – to understand the particular beauty of this construction and not come to hasty conclusions.

Due to reason, using science and technology, humankind constructed a technical monument to the whole planet. To be able to fly, move faster, live better and communicate more quickly with the help of super-technology,

111 d

111 d *Let's not give up!* We shouldn't be afraid of this muddle. It would be easy to run away from this confusing conflict, but that would be cowardice. If we began to shout each other down on the border line, there would be even greater confusion in the picture. We might even fight over the mouse. Calm down! Let's take a closer look at the boundary point.

111 e *We again brought the boundary point closer.* Now it seems that the situation has somewhat calmed down. The red drop is hanging more calmly under the regular yellow arches, but what about those wild black tentacles? (Several friends watched the two artists. The decision was clear. Calm the picture down as much as possible.)

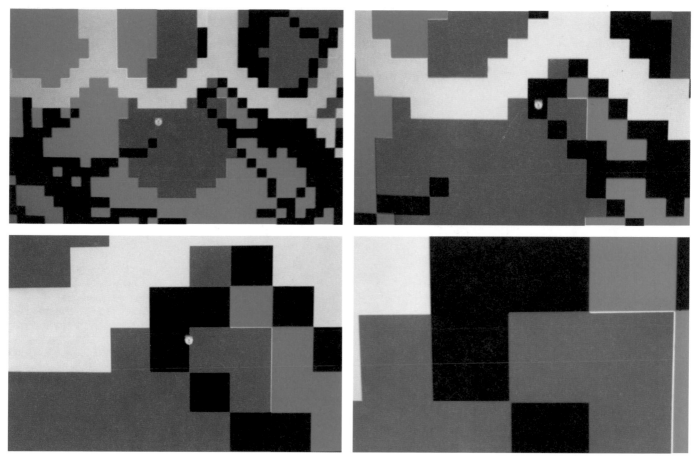

111 e f
g h

111 f *A further enlargement of the detail* proved expedient. The picture calmed down even more, but it seems that the black areas of the original tentacles are pulling the image to the right.

111 g *Even with this enlargement* the children and the two artists were not satisfied.

111 h *Now it's right!* Now it is a balanced picture of agreement. It has the four colours of the original version (111 a). They clearly show the two artists. The agreement is constructive and rational, reflected by the vertical and horizontal lines of the geometric shapes. Every agreement has its order and rules. Don't you agree that many such situations arise every day? We solve them without a computer. The solution of conflict and difference of opinions should not threaten the rights of others.

people transform and exploit the limited natural resources of our planet. Civilisation causes chaos due to its acceleration in cities. We got interesting answers when we asked the children to give examples of confusion and chaos: cars at crossroads, changing TV channels, billboards and advertisements in cities, waste at big dumps and tips, heaps of goods in department stores, antique shops, when people quarrel and cannot reach an agreement. We then tried to draw the confusion and chaos, making a collage but also a graphic mixture from what the computer offered us. When the picture of chaos in front of the children became unbearable, we tried to find out whether it could somehow be put in order and tidied up using artistic creations. Considerations of chaos and order are given on pages 110 and 111.

At the end of the 20th century, humankind knows that its rapid chemical and technical acceleration poisons the soil, rivers, the sea and the air and makes holes in the ozone layer, endangering the ecosystem with the great amount of waste, and severing the natural order of animal and plant species. We also know that if this is not remedied in time, then the slowly ageing globe will be kept alive for the next billion years only by a few micro-organisms. Is it possible to create a material culture and technology that would be in harmony with Nature and not harm it? Are we at all able to come to an agreement? Are we far-sighted enough to recognise that which we should protect and put in order? And what about the Internet, the new information technol-

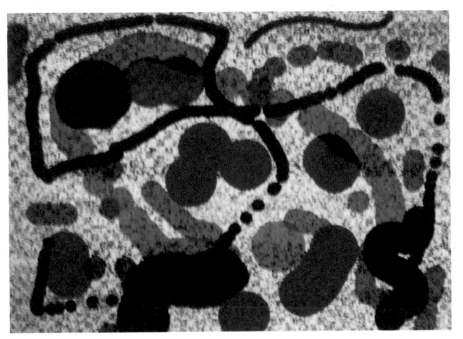

112 a

112 a–f *Calling for help.* On this double page we offer six phases of computer graphics made by a group of children for your consideration. The whole series is based on a vitally important rule: If we don't react to a call for help, the one who calls will die. The one who is calling might be a human being, but may just as well be an endangered animal species (the black stork, a tortoise, a fish) or a plant species; they don't have a strong voice; they don't speak the human language. The children gave the set of images a name: the threat of life in the sea, the sinking of an island, disappearance, how an aquarium died, and the birds will not come back.

112 a *Community.* We are happy playing in a meadow; birds fly around us. Whales in the sea and monkeys in the rainforest could be just as happy.

ogy, which is considered the most revolutionary development in communications? It deals with an unbelievable amount of information, but only the future will show whether the people connected by the Internet will be able to agree on a scale of values and communicate with each other appropriately.

We are giving you at least two artistic series about communication on the computer. The first dialogue, 'How we came to an agreement' on pages 113

112 b

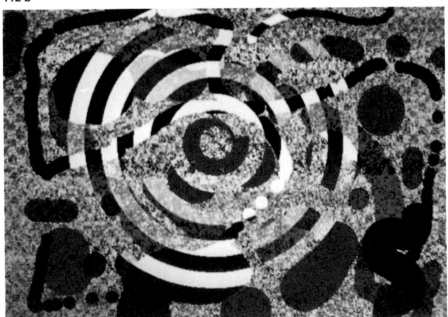

112 b *Danger and calling for help.* Who is calling? Whales? Birds? People? They are endangered but nobody hears them.

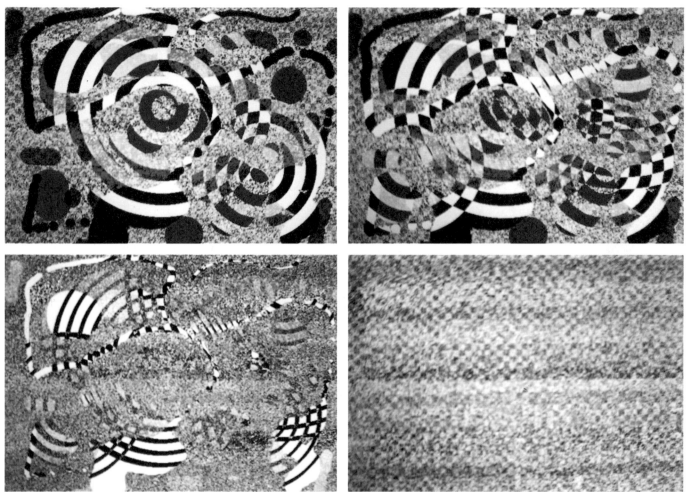

112 c d
e f

112 c, d *The danger has spread.*
More and more animals, plants and
people are calling for help. Perhaps
they are struggling to survive. Nobody
comes to help them. Nobody hears.

112 e, f *The call gets weaker and
stops.* Animals, plants and people
disappear from our environment.
Perhaps only tiny, undefined micro-
organisms survive in the silence that
fills the emptiness. It's too late to ask
what caused the catastrophe if we
didn't discern the call for help in time.

to 115, was conducted by two children. The respective phases are described
in the captions. The second dialogue, 'Calling for help' on pages 116 and
117, originally had more phases than the six given here and was conducted
between the artists and spectators. It is a statement about indifference and
the unwillingness to help. The two series must be read progressively, with
each phase representing a creative agreement between two children. As
there were several alternatives and the pictures printed by the printer were
too slow and expensive for us, it was more convenient to take photographs
of the screen (naturally without a flash). For any further orientation, the photographs could easily be put in line.

What did the children test in these joint activities? They could see whether
they were able to come to an agreement, convince each other of various solutions, appreciate the ideas of the other, praise them and move on. It was
good to come to an agreement about which detail should be enlarged, developed and enlarged again. And so it seems that the picture does not have
a final solution: it branched off into various alternatives and it was possible
to agree on the most interesting. Every child knew which alternative was clos-
est to their heart and was able to call it up from the computer memory.

113 a

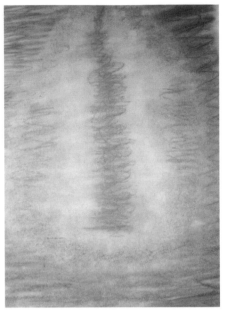

113 b

113 a–c *Lies,* falsehood, untruth, distorted truth, hazy realities, fear and unwillingness to look truth in the eye, to be fooled for a moment ... The children had all this in mind when they made these pictures under the guidance of a student teacher. It was her first job, and she made use of the children returning to an art class after a very open talk on drugs. What will remain of us and what will come after us? No other animal species destroys itself so easily and permanently.

What other subjects could be used for the creative animation of the communications between two or more children? 'What does the human eye see', 'how does the landscape change due to the interference of people or the elements', 'what does a cat think about and what do I think about', 'looking into a crooked mirror', or 'how to get rid of boredom or sadness'.

Whether the children use a pencil, brush or mouse, both individual and collective artworks are worthwhile. In either case, be openly or secretly present

113 c

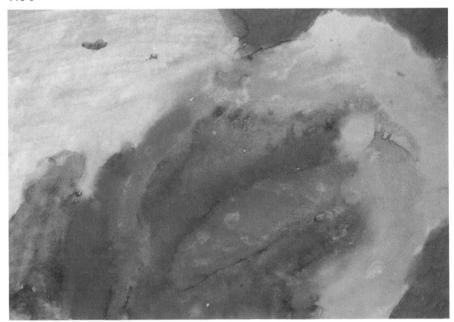

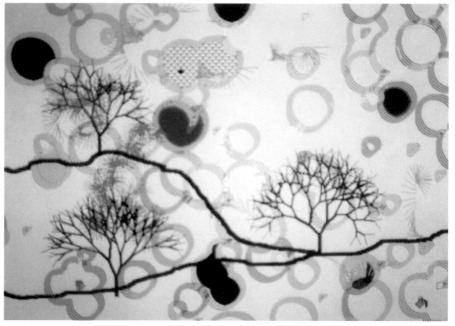

114 a

114 a, b *Spoilt pleasure.* Many things can spoil our mood just as new, white snow can be ruined. It seems as if sorrow, like black soot, has fallen on the once clean computer picture. Everything can be distorted according to our mood, not just the landscape. This is confirmed by various sayings: the world turned grey and pleasure was spoilt. He saw everything as black as if in a broken mirror. The computer graphics program made it possible for the children to express 'spoilt pleasure' in phases. Anything that damages the landscape also changes our mood. The children know a lot about smog and mood changes.

and talk to the children when they draw a landscape in which they feel uneasy, as in pictures 113, 114, 115 and 116. Be with them in the landscapes in which they feel happy, as in pictures 117 and 118. Look at them together.

A person should not be alone. Modern hermits are wrong if they believe that it is sufficient to have the Internet or TV for communication. They are like ants isolated in a comfortable matchbox. An ant cannot survive if it is alone.

114 b

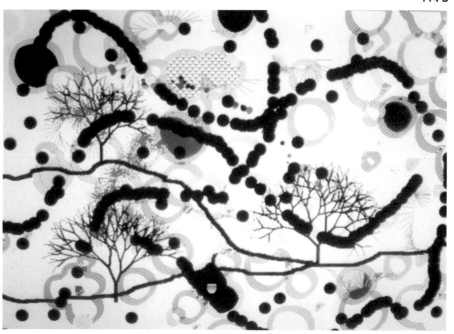

115 a

115 b

115 a–c *Fear.* If we are afraid of something, we should know what it is. It is courageous to confront a 'bogey'. You might find that it was completely unnecessary to be afraid. The fear can be discarded and a friend called to help.

115 a *A spook.* The painting made by a three-year-old boy shows us how a hand courageously chases away a bogey and is not afraid to touch it.

115 b *When I am in fear of darkness*, I always look for someone who will lead me by my hand.

Voluntary hermits in spaceships also know this and must undergo extensive training in preparation for their isolation. Consider this example at the end of our book as a message. The Apollo 13 astronaut hid the tiny, far-away earth with his thumb when he was uncertain as to whether the defective satellite

115 c

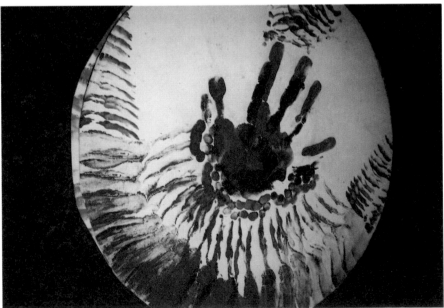

115 c *Beating the drums.* They represent communication. In one school the children pretended to be shamans and magicians. With colours on their hands they first beat a paper like a drum, using a certain rhythm as if they were talking to each other over a distance. They also imagined that they were chasing away evil spirits, fear, bad luck, fire or floods. They gave each other courage.

116 a

116 a, b *Landscapes in which I feel unhappy.* People send each other postcards with lovely scenery when they are travelling, but do you know any dead landscapes with crude oil spilt and heaps of earth from open-pit mines? It' will take years before anything grows there again. It makes you feel sad and shocked: it is the fault of humankind, because we created it. The children tried to imagine a dead country and think of some text to go with it.

116 a *Something wanted to sprout* but the plants are strange. The birds look in vain for a place for their nests. The remains of trees look like lightning. (Distemper painting.)
On the small picture, made by putting a folded foil into a slide frame, we can see 'dead dirt', 'dead water' and poisonous slime. There were more shameful scenes made from a drop of Indian ink and dust. The enlargement of the little picture on a wall evoked surprise.

116 b *A scenery for oil glubbers,* meaning animals which have adjusted to poisonous gases, crude oil, smouldering earth and dead water. The film *Oil Glubbers* was directed by Jan Svěrák. He shot it at the open-pit mines in northern Bohemia. The child's painting reminds us of it.

could be repaired and Apollo 13 return to earth. The astronaut could not communicate with the earth and the ship disappeared on the far side of the moon. At that moment the astronaut realised that home does not mean only one's own house, street, family and friends, and that the feeling of home will last as long as there are people on this planet. He felt that the earth was a miraculous superorganism that should inspire awe. There are conditions for human life connected in unity, in inviolable relations of living and inanimate Nature.

116 b

117 a

117 a *Computer, do you know what apple trees are?* You don't because you are an inanimate grey box. We will try to show you an apple orchard. Even if we put its picture in your memory, you will never know how lovely the orchard is in spring when it blossoms, in summer when it provides shade, and in autumn when the apples turn gold and red.

Just as a person cannot survive alone, so also all of humankind cannot be separated in its super-technical ant-heap, material culture and technology, from the organism of the whole earth. Every animal which would unwisely look for its own advantage and thus unfavourably affect the environment of the other organisms will perish. Errors, mistakes, pride and egoism have to be

117 b

117 b *The way to school?* This is the familiar road which we will remember all our lives. For us it is a happy place. We stop by the houses of our friends and have many experiences and adventures along the way. And so we put its map in the computer memory.

118 a, b *Landscapes where we felt happy*, which we remember and take with us, talk about and look at in photographs. The children drew according to their memories, making things up and re-creating them artistically.

118 a *My holiday lake*. 'There I met many friends and had a lot of fun. I drew all the roads leading from the lake to the surrounding villages.'

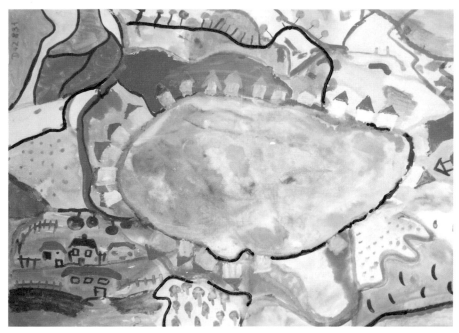

118 a

paid for by the material and spiritual deprivation of the coming generations.

Apollo 13 returned to the earth with its astronaut, so we now know about him and his moment of truth. What will remain of us after the time allotted to every human life? Hopefully a green, blossoming, blue and breathing planet. This is why it is important to care, be informed and able to help.

118 b

118 b *Islands in Greece*. Five-year-old Teresa made these when she came home. On each one there was something interesting. She went for walks with her parents, brothers and sisters and they were all very happy. The countryside is always connected with people. And what about you? Where do you feel happy?

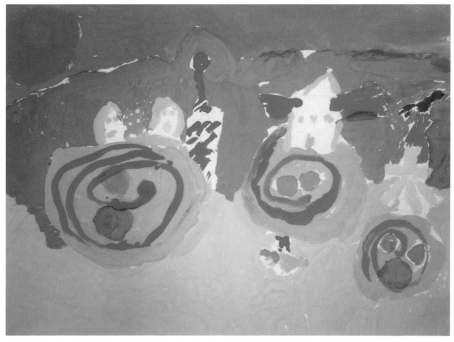

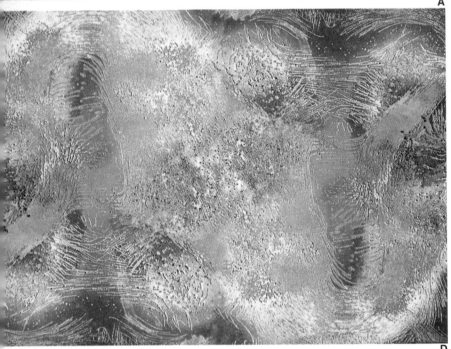

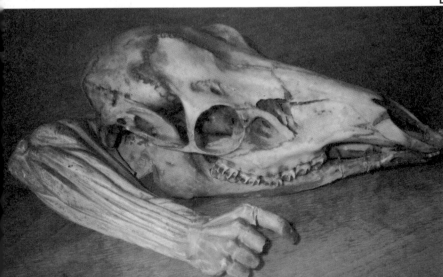

A   Aleš Lamr (born 1943), *The Battle at Troubelice* (Blockhead), 1978, acrylic on canvas, detail from the picture 170 x 120 cm.
Great cruelty, silliness and Gotham-like evil and violence expand and shriek, unable to communicate in any other way, as if the painter did not paint people, but strange parcels.

Funny shapes shout at each other and lament. When will people grow out of their dangerous stupidity?

B *When people quarrel in rage and hatred,* it looks as if they are feeding each other poison. They usually manage to destroy each other. A detail from a student's drawing shows that an artist, too, must show the truth about people, even if it is unpleasant. He chooses such creative means to convince the viewers.

C *When 'all devils are loose',* hell shakes. There is a storm, rain and a strong wind. Two friends found the picture of these devils on the door of an old stove. Where else could you find a picture of hell? Try to paint something similar.

D *A strange still-life.* For students to be able to draw or paint convincingly, they must know anatomy. A parasitic worm is all that is left of a broken model and, grouped together with the skull of an animal, it shows that animals and people are very close in life and death. Let's defend life in all its forms.

E *Anticipation of cohesion.* That ball is hollow, extinct, useless. It is all that remains of a coffee roaster. We must take care of our planet responsibly so that we can survive.

F *A lamp from our grandmother.* How wise the light is that shows others the right path.

G *The road.* Have you recently taken the road you used to walk along as a child? Perhaps it could tell you something interesting. I walked those stairs behind the town walls in Žatec every day since the age of six. Last year I rediscovered them. There was a light on the gate and rails leading up to it. Beyond that gate was a school and the teacher who first taught me to read and write.

H *Bird's-eye view of around Třeboň.* What does the picture at the end of the chapter 'What will Remain of Us?' remind you of? Do you see? A circle, which takes the form of life in an egg or nut, the crown of a tree, a community of friends, a family around a table.

F G

It is also the form of a round planet, the sun with its rays, the galaxies and the universe. If you look closely at the picture you can also see a round face. The nose is the circuit and the mouth are the trees in the green park.

H

A

B

C

A–K *A report on a trip* to the forest one Sunday.
First father found some clay, so they modelled their portraits and decided where to place them:

A, B   Place Mother on the rock.

C   Place Father on the tree stump.

D, E   Five-year-old Teresa once hid among the branches and then in the moss.

F–I   Then they all watched the sun dancing on the logs.

J   Three-year-old Christopher became interested in the fungi. It looks like nests.

K   They took the dry roots home. They are hanging from the ceiling and when they turn their shadows write letters of the forest on the wall.

D

E

F G H I

Every trip offers different inspiration. We put some coloured rosehips and rowan-berries on a dry stalk of grass, looked for fantastic statues of rocks or stones in the image of people or animals. Why not put a 'forest man' made of bark, twigs, cones and grass on a tree stump, or make a picture on a piece of paper like a kind of music sheet for the voice of the forest? What colour is the voice of the jay or magpie? Or we should look quietly then close our eyes and talk about the nice things we can recall.

K

J

ACKNOWLEDGEMENTS
The Publishers would like to thank all
the artists for having provided the pictorial
material used in this book.